THE MAKINGS OF *Peace*

SPIRITUAL AND PSYCHOLOGICAL FOUNDATIONS
FOR LIVING AT PEACE
WITH GOD, YOURSELF AND OTHERS

Lenore T. Gray

The Makings Of Peace: Spiritual and Psychological Foundations for Living at Peace with God, Yourself and Others

Illustrated graphics by Andrea Astes

ISBN: 979-8-218-96326-2

Table of Contents

Acknowledgements

THERE ARE MANY people who have encouraged me and prayed for me through the years while I have been writing this book. I want to thank Holy Spirit especially for nudging me and reminding me to write. I also want to apologize to Him for all the times I ignored His promptings or was afraid to continue in the endeavor. I am trusting that in spite of my procrastination and fears He will be able to use this book for His purposes.

I also want to thank the following people for reviewing the manuscript, editing it, and making suggestions: Candy Willut, Marcella Shadle, and Bob and Sandy Massey.

Others who have been faithful to pray are Dani and David Sprinkle, Matt and Ashley Gray, Jim and Candy Willut, Kent and Marcia Bickle, and my church family at Grace Bible Fellowship in Keller, Texas. I know there are others who have prayed for me as well. Thank you.

Preface

EVERY MINUTE OF our lives we are working to be at peace. Right this minute as you read this text, you are trying to be at peace on some level. Are you comfortable (at peace) in the way you are sitting, standing, etc.? Are you reading one more self-help book in search for the nugget that will set your heart at ease? Are you searching for some sort of spiritual Nirvana that will baptize your whole life with bliss? Be it implicitly or explicitly, we are searching for peace.

Homeostasis. Balance. Peace.

Merriam-Webster's Collegiate Dictionary defines peace as

> a state of tranquility or quiet, freedom from civil disturbance; a state of security or order within a community provided for by law or custom; freedom from disquieting or oppressive thoughts or emotions; harmony in personal relations; a state or period of mutual concord between governments, a pact or agreement to end hostilities between those who have been at war or in a state of enmity. [It can be] used interjectionally to ask for silence or calm or as a greeting or farewell — at peace : in a state of concord or tranquility.[1]

Imagine what it would be like to have Webster's definition in place in your personal life, in your community, in your country, in your world.

It is safe to say that as long as human nature is at play, the peace Webster defines will never exist. We live in a world where everything is broken because of Adam's folly. By "everything", I mean every last particle of creation: everything from the stars to all of the earth, to our hearts and souls. The New Testament Book of Romans 8:21 says "creation itself also will be delivered from the bondage of corruption..." Fortunately, Jesus has come to bring healing to all the brokenness. Because of Him, the Prince of Peace, we have hope of relative peace here on earth and perfect peace in heaven.

As humans we are creatures of three parts: spirit, soul and body. To be in perfect peace, it is necessary for each component of our being to be running smoothly or working in a manner that is consistent with how we are created. So what does that look like? Well, the details are different for everyone, since we are all created differently for a specific purpose that is uniquely our own. However, there are a few general concepts that apply to everyone. This little book is not meant to be the encyclopedia for peace, but a stepping-off place into a life that is in tune with your Creator, your fellow earth-travelers, and your self.

This book will touch on things that make for peace in the three aspects of humanness. The first aspect I will address is spirit, the ethereal/eternal part of us that drives everything about the rest of us. My training and experience is in Christian and biblical theology, so the premise of this writing is based on the Christian worldview and the Bible. The second topic is soul, which will be defined as our mind, will and emotions. I have formal training and years of experience as a clinical counselor. My hope is that the gleanings from my years of experience and training may be helpful to anyone who reads this. Thirdly, I'll talk about the body, which is the material part of our existence—sort of the vehicle we have been provided to haul the rest of our existence around. I am not a nutritionist, nor a kinesthesiologist, nor a physician of any kind. What I will provide is a few biblical references, and some insights that will encourage you to take care of your vehicle.

We are "fearfully and wonderfully made." As humans, we are the pinnacle of creation—the pinnacle of a gloriously magnificent masterpiece created by the most glorious of all Persons. We are made in the image of that Person. We are made in the image of God. Our primary purpose in life is to enhance His reputation. Period. As a person, when we create something, we want it to communicate something about who we are that evokes admiration. It is the same with God. We live in a fallen, broken world. Until we reach heaven, where there is no corruption, we will have only glimpses of living in perfect peace. We have no peace when we look to a fallen broken world for peace, because we were not created to live in a fallen, broken world; we were created for paradise. However, since this world is our portal into life, we can purpose to live in such a way that gives evidence that our Creator is smarter, wiser, more powerful, more (fill in the blank with anything except evil) than anything or anyone in all the rest of creation.

NOTES

[1]Frederick C. Mish ed., *Merriam-Webster's Collegiate® Dictionary, Tenth Edition*, (Merriam-Webster, Inc., Springfield, MA, USA, 2000), p. 852.

PART I

Spirit

Thou hast made us for thyself, O Lord, and our heart is restless until it finds its rest in thee.

AUGUSTINE OF HIPPO

Introduction

THERE IS ONLY one place in the Bible that mentions "perfect peace" or *shalom shalom*:

"You [God] will keep him in perfect peace,
Whose mind is stayed on You, because he trusts in You."
(Isaiah 26:3, New King James Version (NKJV))

Strong's Concordance describes this Hebrew *shalom* word as "completeness, wholeness, peace, health, welfare, safety, soundness, tranquility, prosperity, perfectness, fullness, rest, harmony, absence of agitation or discord."[1] *Shalom* comes from the word *shalam*, which means to be complete, perfect, and full. "Thus *shalom* is much more than the absence of war and conflict; it is the wholeness that the entire human race seeks."[2]

The context of Isaiah 26:3 mentioned above is the 8th century BC during Isaiah the prophet's ministry in Judah. During this time Israel was being attacked by a powerful enemy. Isaiah counseled against reliance on outside help from either Assyria or Egypt. However, Isaiah's clear warnings against participating in international power politics and his admonitions to rely only on the Lord were ignored. Israel and eventually Judah were taken into exile. The Temple, Israel's cultural and religious center, was destroyed. The people were deported to Babylon and became serfs of their fiercest enemy. The message of the Book of Isaiah is that God is the author of history—past, present and future—and that He is in control of everything, even the actions of the hated empires and enemies. Chapters 24-27 of Isaiah contrast two cities: one (possibly Babylon) is symbolic of or a composite of cities under judgment. The second is the future Jerusalem, the city under the rule of Messiah,[3] the man-God who was sent by God to save creation from the ravages of sin and bring perfect peace to those who trust in him.

Circumstances were dire for Judah and Israel with their strong enemies bearing down on them. In the midst of impossible circumstances, Isaiah counseled to trust in the Lord for rescue and perfect peace. Isaiah was indicating that Israel could experience not only the end of political hostilities, but inner tranquility and a sense of complete wholeness.

There is nothing new under the sun (Eccl. 1:9). Circumstances in the United States and the world aren't much different now in 2023 than they were in the time of Isaiah. As in Isaiah's time, the answer is found in trusting in the Lord. More specifically for our time, the answer is Jesus, the Prince of Peace. In Him we have *shalom* and the hope of *shalom shalom* (perfect peace).

Jesus'/Messiah's principal purpose is to bring reconciliation between humankind and God. Jesus promised His followers, "My peace I give to you..." (New Testament Book of John 14:27). The New Covenant, the contractual agreement that He came to establish, was introduced through the prophet Jeremiah in the early part of the 7th century BCE:

> "...I [God] will put My laws in their minds and write them on their hearts; and I will be their God and they shall be My people. [33] No more shall every man teach his neighbor, and every man his brother, saying, 'Know the Lord,' for all shall know Me, from the least of them to the greatest of them, says the Lord. For I will forgive their iniquity, and their sin I will remember no more" [34] (Isaiah, 31:33b-34, NKJV).

So, what are God's laws? Why do we need them at all? Why do we need them "written on our hearts", and what does that mean? What does it mean to "know God?"

NOTES:

[1]James Strong, *Strong's Exhaustive Concordance of the Bible, Hebrew and Chaldee Dictionary, 42nd Ed.*, (Abingdon Press, 1983, #7965), p. 116.

[2]Jack W. Hayford, Ed., *Hayford's Bible Handbook*, (Thomas Nelson, Inc., Nashville, TN, 1995), p. 716.

[3]Michael D. Coogan, Ed., *New Oxford Annotated Bible, Third Edition*, (Oxford University Press, Oxford, NY, 2001), p. 975.

CHAPTER 1

God's Guardrails

Why We Need the Law

IN ORDER TO understand the need for law, it is important to understand the etymology of human nature. In the Judeo/Christian Bible, God spoke and all of creation came into being including the first two humans. God named them Adam and Eve and placed them in an idyllic paradise called the Garden of Eden. Here they had perfect relationship with each other and with God. God told them they could eat of all the fruit of the Garden except the tree of the knowledge of good and evil. The devil (evil embodied and God's enemy), disguised himself as a serpent, lied to Eve and convinced her that eating the forbidden fruit would be okay. In fact, it would make her like God. Eve in turn convinced Adam to have some of the fruit. And so they disobeyed God and introduced evil/sin into creation. As a result, death was introduced and all of creation was corrupted. Adam and Eve were no longer innocent. They had acquired the knowledge that in the world there exists good and evil. They could now judge themselves and all of creation. And they found themselves wanting. They hid from God and tried to cover their shame with fig leaves. Moreover, and more catastrophic than that, because of their decision to disobey God, Adam and Eve were separated from God, cast out of paradise, and their relationship with each other was contaminated as well. Unfortunately, this brokenness, which orthodox Christianity calls original sin, is passed down through DNA and the spirit to all of Adam and Eve's descendants. All of humankind is plagued with sin and death. Adam and Eve, and all of us humans by inheritance, are broken so deeply that we no longer have the capacity to live in a way that aligns with how we were created and therefore be acceptable to our Creator. Left to our own devices, we become destructive to ourselves, each other, and our environment. We need some guardrails. We need the Law. Law works best if it is part of our moral code, culture and the way we view and operate in life—i.e. written on our hearts. Without that, it feels like harsh tyrannical restrictions and oppression.

In every culture there are rules (laws) that dictate how to do life. These rules are written, unwritten, spoken, assumed. They are everything from legislated and policed laws to etiquette and body language. Without some sort of organization society devolves into chaos and anarchy. Evil thrives in chaos. In chaos we become desperate for peace and will abandon established morality and social mores in order to establish or re-establish peace. Saul D. Alinsky, a 20th century change agent, teaches his followers to "engage in large scale social engineering, attempting to unfreeze a society using chaos, and to then refreeze it in a new predefined shape."[1] While these tactics are effective, they are ungodly. In 1 Corinthians 14:33 (New Testament letter) Paul writes that "...God is not the author of confusion, but of peace..."

A lawyer once asked Jesus, "'Which is the great commandment in the law?' Jesus said to him, 'You shall love the Lord your God with all your heart, with all your soul, and with all your mind. This is the first and great commandment. And the second is like it: You shall love your neighbor as yourself. On these two commandments hang all the Law and the Prophets'" (Matthew 22:37-40). In other words, the Law's primary purpose is to set a foundation for reestablishing a peaceful, loving relationship with God and with each other.

> "...the law was given as an essential meeting place between God and humans beings in covenant relationship with him, where the sincere heart would be received, instructed, and enabled by God to walk in his ways. God is the only restorer of souls. When those walking in personal relationship with him take his law into their heart, that law, as a living principle, quickens and restores connection and order to the flagging

soul. ... Spirit, covenant, and law always go hand in hand within the path of spiritual formation, for it is the path of one who walks with God."[2] Dallas Willard

"God" is YHWH, the God of the Judeo/Christian Bible, "the Father, the Almighty, maker of heaven and earth, of all that is, seen and unseen."[3]

God gave the Law to the nation Israel through the prophet/ leader, Moses. It is contained in the first five books of the Hebrew Bible known as the Torah. There are 613 laws in the transcript covering every aspect of life including, but not limited to, what you eat, how to do business, whom you marry, and how to worship and follow YHWH. Fortunately, because of Jesus, His disciples are not required to follow many of them (see the New Testament letter from Paul to the Colossians, Chapter 3 verses 16-19). Please note that Jesus did not come to abolish the Law, but to fulfill it.[3] Some of the Law still applies to anyone who wants to live in peace. Rather than parsing out the laws, which address the civil and ceremonial aspects of their culture, I want to focus on the moral laws known as the Ten Commandments. These laws describe how we are meant to live in relation with God and each other. They don't address any type of punishment. If we all lived by the letter and the spirit of these laws, no police force or punishment would be necessary. We could all live in harmony.

The Ten Commandments are numbered a little differently in Roman Catholic versus Protestant traditions. The difference lies in the law against covetousness (10th Commandment) and how the First and Second Commandments are delineated. See Exodus 20:4-17 (Old Testament in the Bible) for the passage where Moses speaks them to Israel. For the most part, there is little difference in substance according the Roman Catholic teaching, and Protestants say the difference is significant. I'm not here to argue doctrine. I'll use the Protestant version, since Catholics say it doesn't matter that much.[5]

According to most Protestant and Jewish traditions the Ten Commandments are:

1. I am the Lord your God. You shall have no other gods before me.
2. You shall not make for yourself an idol.
3. Do not take the name of the Lord in vain.
4. Remember the Sabbath and keep it holy.
5. Honor your father and mother.
6. You shall not kill/murder.
7. You shall not commit adultery.
8. You shall not steal.
9. You shall not bear false witness against your neighbor.
10. You shall not covet your neighbor's spouse or anything that belongs to your neighbor.

The first four commandments have to do with our relationship with God and how we are to honor and respect Him. The last six are instruction on how we are to treat our fellow earth travelers. Let's take a brief look at each one.

1. I am the Lord your God. You shall have no other gods before me.

This Commandment says that there is only one true God (i.e., the God, YHWH of the Judeo/Christian Bible). To worship anything or anyone else puts you outside the guardrails of the law. Anything that is worshipped besides the true God is an idol. Unfortunately, absolutely anything can be an idol. Anything or anyone that we believe we can't live without (except God Himself) is an idol. Tim Keller in his book *Gospel in Life* has a good chapter on idolatry. Some types of idolatry that he lists are power, approval, comfort, control, helping, dependence, independence, work, achievement, materialism, religion, individual persons, irreligion, race/culture, popularity, family, relationships, suffering, ideology, and image. You can see that many of these are good; but if the need for them outstrips the love of God, they become idols—an instrument to rob you of true peace.[6] "To the extent that God is exalted in the minds of people, and his very name is cherished with utmost respect, everything else goes right."[7] Martin Luther said this about the First Commandment:

> All those who do not at all times trust God and do not in all their works or sufferings, life and death, trust in His favor, grace and goodwill, but seek His favor in other things or in themselves, do not keep this [First] Commandment, and practice real idolatry, even if they were to do the works of all the other commandments, and in addition had all the prayers, fasting, obedience, patience, chastity, and innocence of all the saints combined. For the chief work is not present, without which all the others are nothing but mere sham, show and pretence.[8]

If you don't worship God, it doesn't matter how "good" you are, you are missing the essential point of morality and life.

Humans are born with a need to know or believe that there is a higher power. Children who are as young as three years old have exhibited the longing for relationship with a "transcendent other"[9]. Biblical writers knew this hundreds of years before Jesus. The first and most important commandment merely agrees with how we humans are created. We live in peace when we are living according to how we are created. Living in relationship and loving a transcendent other, or God, is a key element of living in peace.

2. You shall not make for yourself an idol.

This commandment at its foundation warns against trying to control every aspect of our lives—including the inexplicable (e.g., why does one person get hired for a job and another person doesn't when their background, experience and personality are virtually identical?). The historical context of Israel was one in which the cultures had a god for everything in order to make sense of the unanswerable (e.g., making abeyance to the god of fertility when your wife is having trouble conceiving). By doing something that will influence the god, you can change your circumstances, get your way, be in control. If one can make an image or even a symbol of God, one is taking the first step in controlling Him. God is ALL powerful and in absolute control of everything. He limits Himself (i.e., doesn't always intervene and control everything) when it comes to human will and choices in order to engage in authentic love with us. He doesn't want robots; He wants a love relationship. However, He can control human will, if He sees fit. "The heart of the king is in the hand of the Lord." (See Deut 2:30, Ezra 6:22, and especially Proverbs 21:1). God is supreme in all aspects of life and creation—even aspects that we do not have the capacity to understand. To consider Him as anything else is to put something else in that place of supremacy. Using symbolism for communication purposes regarding God is not sin in itself. E.g. using the word "God." The problem is using the symbol to limit Him within the scope of the symbol.[10]

In practice, the 2nd Commandment addresses the fact that the righteous (the morally upright or good) live by faith (trust in and reliance on God). True worship of the living God is done through trust and dependence on a Being we cannot see or understand completely. John Wesley says, "[The 2nd Commandment] forbids us to make images of God in our fancies, as if He were a man as we are. Our religious worship must be governed by the power of faith, not by the power of imagination."[11] Wesley goes on to say that we cannot use any sort of image to enter into worship. The Bible is replete with anthropomorphic references to God such as the hand of God, His eyes, His heart, etc. This reference is for the reader's sake to help him/her identify with God and understand on a very simple level how God operates. However, God $\neq$ humans x holiness^n or oceans x power^n. God doesn't fit into any equation that we can conjure up. He is outside of creation, and therefore outside our imaginations and sources of reference including mathematics and science. The anthropomorphic references are depictions of God that are dumbed down more than we can imagine. God's passion to be in relationship with humans requires Him to come down to our level in order to communicate with us and help us to experience His presence and love for us.

3. Do not take the name of the Lord in vain.

It is common to think of this commandment in terms of not using God's or Jesus' name as a swear word (e.g., "Oh God!" or "Jesus Christ!"). According to Strong's Concordance, the word translated as "vain" implies devastation, destruction, uselessness, degradation.[12] In other words do not use the Lord's name in a way that causes destruction to His name. "Name" does not only indicate His moniker, but His authority and character as well.[13] Using God's name in a flippant, offhanded way disrespects Him, which is the heart of the 3rd Commandment.

I find it interesting that so many swear words invoke God. Why not invoke, say, cabbage? If everyone knew cabbage references meant high emotionality, wouldn't it catch on? I doubt it. Referencing cabbage doesn't degrade God. The word "f-ck" seems to be a popular swear word these days. The shock value comes partly from sexual innuendo. Another aspect of this word is that the sexual act, particularly between a man and a woman is representative of God. During the Creation narrative in Genesis 1:26-28 God says,

> "Let Us make man in Our image, according to Our likeness; let them have dominion ... over all the earth and over every creeping thing that creeps on the earth. So God created man in His own image; in the image of God He created him; male and female He created them. Then God blessed them, and God said to them, "Be fruitful and multiply; fill the earth and subdue it; have dominion over ... every living thing that moves on the earth."

According to this passage, humankind is the image of God in creation. Moreover, "Be fruitful and multiply" implies have sex and make babies. The union between a man and a woman represents God more than anything else in creation. To degrade that act by using a word for it as a swear word or engaging in the act flippantly or perversely (i.e., outside traditional marriage, which is a life-long commitment between a man and a woman that is sanctioned by their community) is to degrade the image of God. Ephesians 5:1-13 admonishes us to be imitators of God. Represent Him faithfully and not by engaging in "filthiness, or foolish talking, nor coarse jesting, but rather giving of thanks."

4. Remember the Sabbath to keep it holy.

The 4th Commandment was instituted to put aside one day in seven to rest and contemplate the things of God. One day to completely focus on Him. It was designed not just for our spiritual well-being and connection with God, but for our physical and psychological/emotional well-being as well.

On the seventh day of Creation, God "rested from all His work" (Exodus 20). He took some time to admire His handiwork—all the things that He had made and said were "good" and "very good". Having been made in His image, we are to do the same—take some time to contemplate and admire the things of God: creation, His blessings toward us, how He is moving in our lives, etc. By stopping the busyness of life and being present with God, each other and our world, enormous emotional and spiritual benefit is garnered. It is an invitation to truly rest and enter into *shabbat shalom* (perfect peace).

> "God not only appointed the seventh day, but he blessed it. It is not only a day of honour to God, but a day of blessing to us; it is not only a day wherein we give God worship, but a day wherein he gives us grace. On this day a blessing drops down from heaven. God himself is not benefited by it, we cannot add one cubit to his essential glory; but we ourselves are benefited. This day, religiously observed, entails a blessing upon our souls, our estate, and our posterity."[14] Thomas Watson

The passage in Exodus regarding the 4th Command says, " [the] Lord blessed the sabbath day, and hallowed it." As we enter into the Sabbath, we enter into the blessing. By taking time to connect with God and with each other we engage in forms of attachment, an important emotional stabilizer, which plays an important part in the development of morality and sense of self. (See Appendix 1 for a more extensive conversation about attachment.) By taking time to enumerate our blessings, we practice gratitude, a powerful antidote to depression. My own experience is that a Sunday afternoon nap just makes the week go better.

There is some controversy regarding which day of the week God wants us to celebrate Sabbath: Sunday or Saturday. In the Creation narrative in Genesis 2, the days of the week are not delineated. The passage merely says that God rested from His work and blessed/hallowed the seventh day. In Exodus 20:11 (For [in] six days the LORD made heaven and earth, the sea, and all that in them [is], and rested the seventh day: wherefore the LORD blessed the sabbath day and hallowed it.) Where the commandment is first established, the word "Sabbath" essentially means to take a break, an "intermission". There are those who believe that adherence to the 4th Commandment means observing it on Saturday, the seventh day of the week in the Gregorian calendar. They have a problem with observing it on Sunday. Nowhere in Scripture is the day of rest changed. Even though the apostles broke bread and met together on the first day of the week vs. the last day, the commandment was never abrogated. In 321 A.D. Constantine made a political move in the newly conquered pagan lands and pronounced the official day of worship for everyone to be Sunday, the day named for their sun god.[15] Wilson goes on to explain that Jesus rose from the dead on the first day of the week. Moreover, Pentecost, the day Jesus sent the Holy Spirit in power, happened on the first day of the week. Thomas Watson concludes this: "The reason why God instituted the old Sabbath was to be a memorial of the creation; but he has now brought the first day of the week in its room in memory of a more glorious work than creation, which is redemption. ... **The morality or substance of the fourth commandment does not lie in keeping the**

seventh day precisely, but keeping one day in seven is what God has appointed."[16] In light of Jesus' statement that the Sabbath was made for man and not man for the Sabbath (Mark 2:27), I agree with Watson. The heart of the commandment calls us to set aside one day in seven for God, to connect with Him and rest.

Keep in mind that the commandments are not for God's benefit but for ours. For God to exist, He doesn't need humans. He doesn't need anything. He is self-sufficient and exists apart from all creation. He tells us to keep Him at the center of our lives and the head of our affections because He knows we need a morally superlative spiritual being outside and above ourselves to continually call us out of our brokenness and animalistic tendencies. When we deny God's existence or ignore His authority, we tend to spiral into animal behavior or worse.

As you can see from these first four commandments, God is serious about humans keeping Him in the highest place of authority, respect, affection and consideration in their hearts and lives. We are made in His image and represent Him in the earth. When we fall short of that glory, we dishonor God and His enemy, the devil and/or personification of evil, delights it. Having established the supremacy of God and our place in relation to Him in the first four commandments, the last six commandments tell us how to treat each other.[17]

5. Honor your father and mother.

The full text of the 5th Commandment is "Honor your father and mother, that your days may be long upon the land which the Lord your God is giving you" (Exodus 20:12, NKJV). This is the first command with a promise—long life in a place set apart specifically for you. The operative word here is "honor." The Hebrew word translated here is *kabad* or *kabed*: a prim. root; to be severe, heavy, i.e. in a bad sense *(burdensome, severe, dull)* or in a good sense *(numerous, rich, honorable)*.[18]

If your parents were bad or you had a bad attitude toward them, they would be, or you would treat them as, "burdensome, severe, dull." If your parents were good or you had a good attitude toward them, you would treat them as "numerous, rich, honorable." I think it is safe to say that the God of love wants us to have a good attitude toward each other. With the 5th Commandment He puts emphasis on treating our parents with respect.

Our parents are the most influential people in our lives for all of our lives. They lay the foundations of mental, emotional, moral, and spiritual well-being and identity. These foundations heavily influence every aspect of our lives. They are our mentors in culture. The promise of the commandment, "that your days may be long upon the land, which the Lord your God is giving you," is connected to creating a culture in the land, passing along behaviors and traditions, skills and narratives that establish a people group. This commandment calls us to recognize the weight of their position as life givers and culture sustainers.[19]

As infants and children we look to our parents for provision, guidance, acceptance, love, identity, etc. In a real sense, they are like gods to us. No parent is perfect. It is a watershed moment in the journey to maturity to recognize that our parents are not God and that we cannot expect them to fulfill all of our needs. By recognizing the weight of their influence, we can decide to embrace the good and/or reject the bad. We can learn to be grateful for what they did give us, even if it is to recognize that they are God's avenue for giving us life on this earth and an opportunity for eternal life and glory. We can also learn to forgive them for what they couldn't provide.

The position of this commandment is significant. It is between those commandments that tell us how to treat God and those that tell us how to treat each other. Parents hold the position of god for the formative years of life. We are to honor them for that. As we mature we recognize their humanness, their fallibilities and weaknesses, and ideally turn our worship to God Himself. In the meantime, our parents teach us how to honor and recognize authority and live in humility—or not.

6. You shall not kill/murder.

The word "kill" is translated from the Hebrew word *ratsach* (to dash in pieces, i.e., kill (a human being), espec. to murder;—to put to death, kill).[20] "This commandment forbids murder, not the forms of killing authorized for Israel such as war and capital punishment."[20] That sounds simple enough: don't kill each other. However, Jesus in Matthew 5:20-21 takes this command a step further.

Remember, Jesus came not to abolish the law but to write it on our hearts—make it our primary desire and moral compulsion. He says in Matthew 5:20 "For I tell you, unless your righteousness exceeds that of the scribes and Pharisees, you will never enter the kingdom of heaven." He goes on regarding the 6th Commandment,

> "You have heard that it was said to those of ancient times, "You shall not murder'; and 'whoever murders shall be liable to judgment.' But I say to you that if you are angry with a brother or sister, you will be liable to judgment; and if you insult a brother or sister, you will be liable to the council; and if you say, 'You fool,' you will be liable to the hell of fire. So when you are offering your gift at the altar, if you remember that your brother or sister has something against you, [24]leave your gift there before the altar and go; first to be reconciled to your brother or sister, and then come and offer your gifts." NRSV

The word "angry" is translated from the Greek word *orgizo (orgidzo)*:

> to provoke or enrage, i.e. (pass.) become exasperated;—be angry (wroth). (Strongs Concordance 3710). Taken from 3709. orge; prop. desire as a reaching forth or excitement of the mind), i.e. (by anal.) violent passion (ire, or [justifiable] abhorrence); by impl. punishment;—anger, indignation, vengeance, wrath.[22]

In his letter to the Ephesians Paul says, "Be angry, and do not sin; do not let the sun go down on your wrath" (Eph 4:26, NKJV). In the NRSV the passage is footnoted to point out that Paul is referencing Psalm 4:4. A couple of translations are: "When you are disturbed, do not sin" (NRSV). And my personal favorite, "Don't sin by letting anger control you" (New Living Translation).

Anger is a secondary emotion. That is, when you feel anger there is another emotion driving the anger (e.g., betrayal, injustice, indignation, pride, hopelessness, helplessness, etc.). By simply naming the emotion, you decrease the intensity of the emotion.[23] If we don't name the emotion driving the anger we stay in a heightened emotional state, which often has no constructive purpose. Moreover, the intense emotion can literally shut down the logical brain. The anger itself is not the problem. The 6th Commandment is broken when you let the anger control your behavior in a way that harms others and disrupts relationships.

Usually, some kind of fear-based belief is driving your need to rise up and defend yourself. This could be a legitimate fear, or it could be some holdover from an earlier time in your life, such as a belief that no longer is true for you, or a misunderstanding conceived by you as a child. It could have been someone calling you a derogatory name and you internalized it. In a child's mind, being told something like, "You fool!" could be translated as, "You're worthless/unloveable!", especially if he/she hears it repeated with intensity or in anger. A statement like that from the right person in the right context can literally cripple a person emotionally. In extreme cases, the result can be suicide. Ultimately, of course, the death of the person committing suicide is the choice of the one killing herself/himself. However, our words can wound and cause emotional/mental destruction. That is what Jesus is warning against: being a destructive force in someone's life. Killing the body is one thing. Damaging (killing) the soul or spirit is worthy of the same punishment. In the eyes of the One who created us, every part of us is precious and deserves to be valued. [See Appendix 2 for the Reactive Cycle Fear Dance, a tool to help you determine what is driving your heightened emotion (e.g., fears and lies you are believing)].

7. You shall not commit adultery.

"Commit adultery" is the English translation for the Hebrew word *na'aph.*[24] Adultery is having sex as a married person with a person you are not married to or having sex with a married person you are not married to.

The subject of sexual purity could fill an entire library. Suffice it to say, in biblical writings the only time sex is approved is between one man and one woman in a committed relationship that is sanctioned by their community. Period. When two people come together in intercourse, Jesus said that the two become one flesh (Matt. 19:5, referencing Gen 2:24). "Flesh" is the translation for the Greek word *sarx*, which means the meat of the body or human nature (the soul) with all its frailties and passions.[25] You also become one with every other person that person ever had sex with. A person who has multiple sex partners becomes fragmented and invaded physically, emotionally, and spiritually.

Sexual intercourse between a man and a woman in marriage is a sacred moment. The purpose of every part of Creation, including and especially humans, is to represent God at His best. We humans are made in His image and therefore represent Him in Creation more perfectly than anything else. In Genesis 1:27-28 the creation narrative says:

> So God created humankind in his image, in the image of God he created them; male and female he created them. God blessed them and God said to them, "Be fruitful and multiply..." (NRSV).

In other words, come together and create new life. This creation of new life looks more like God and glorifies Him more than anything else in Creation. It is confined to marriage for the physical, emotional and spiritual protection of the participants.

8. You shall not steal.

Don't claim or take for your own what is not legitimately yours or given to you. Objects are not the only things that can be stolen. Some examples are:

Time: Your employer pays you a certain amount of money per hour to work for his/her business enterprises. If you spend that time doing something other than the work you were hired for (e.g., playing games, using social media, non-work-related texting), you are stealing time from your employer.

Authority: I once took my son to the doctor for an ear infection. I mentioned something about the necessity to take all of the antibiotic that was prescribed. Instead of talking directly to me and correcting me, the doctor turned to my child and told him I was wrong, he didn't need to take it all. The doctor stole my parental authority. (By the way, the doctor was wrong. Needless to say, I never went back to that doctor.)

Attention: It's your birthday. Instead of celebrating you, your sibling acts out and steals the show and the acknowledgement/attention that belonged to you.

9. You shall not bear false witness against your neighbor.

Don't lie. Do not intentionally speak or say anything other than what you know to be absolutely true. A half-truth is the same as a lie. Manipulation is a type of lying—telling a story or giving your opinion without telling the whole story in order to serve your agenda.

Unintentionally relating disinformation is not lying. I once said I was going to bring a chicken dish to a gathering of friends. When I went to the store to purchase the chicken, the store was out of chicken. I brought a fish dish to the party instead. One of the people at the gathering said, "So you lied." When I initially said I would bring chicken, I was relating my honest intention. If I had said I would bring chicken knowing full well at that moment that no chicken was available and I would bring fish instead, that would have been a lie. As it was, I was mistaken in assuming that the store would have chicken.

It is common these days to hear people say something to the effect, "We all have our own truth." It is a subtle notion of relativism. We all have our own *reality*. We all have a unique way of viewing our world based on our cultural environment, experiences, choices, etc. The fact is, if there is no truth above opinion, there is no truth at all. Truth is uncorrupted reality in the frame of perfect wisdom. In and of itself, creation cannot hold truth, because creation is corrupted. Our human reality is corrupted, and only God has perfect wisdom because only He understands and is cognizant of every aspect of creation. We only get truth when God breaks into creation with His understanding and reality. Jesus said, "I am the way, the TRUTH, and the life" (John 14:6). He broke into creation with perfect understanding of us and of God.

10. You shall not covet ... anything that is your neighbor's.

The Hebrew word translated "covet" is *chamad (khaw-mad').* It means to greatly delight in or lust after something. Webster defines covet: "to wish for enviously" or "to feel inordinate desire for what belongs to another."[26] I imagine we have all been envious of someone else's possessions or position. The operative word in the definition is "inordinate" (i.e., immoderate or excessive). When we obsess about another person's belongings or take steps to make the object our own, then it is coveting. It is the heart condition that is present before one steals.

The mature approach to guard against covetousness is to turn your thoughts away from the actual desirable object and consider ways you can acquire something similar. How can you work harder, save more or meet someone, etc. Consider what you have to be thankful for. Look for ways to improve what you do have, or learn to be content with it if improvement is outside your means.

Jesus and the Law

The problem is that our broken human nature makes it impossible to follow the law perfectly. Israel tried to follow the Law for 3,000 years before Christ without success. Our highest level of thinking and doing right (or righteousness) doesn't measure up to God's parameters for behavior and attitude. As a matter of fact, the law only makes it more evident how weak and imperfect we are and exacerbates our tendency to feel shame. That's where Jesus comes in.

Nearly every culture on the planet has some sort of system for making up for wrongdoing or alleviating shame. The penal system is an example. A criminal does time in jail or prison for crimes to fulfill his/her debt to society, to "pay for sin," to use Judeo/Christian vernacular. Roman Catholic doctrine teaches that one can pray or do penance for cleansing from sins. In Buddhist teaching atonement is reached through reincarnation and living a lesser life until you get it right, earning good Karma until you finally reach eternal bliss. Most pagan belief systems are based on ways to appease the god in charge. In ancient Judaism animals and grains were burned on the altar of their house of worship as offerings for sin. In continuation of the Jewish tradition, Jesus presented Himself to God the Father as the final offering for sin (Hebrews 10:1-18). By accepting the sacrifice of Jesus, who never sinned and was therefore a perfect sacrifice (2 Corinthians 5:21 and 1 John 2:2), choosing to give up a life of sinfulness to follow Jesus, and believing that this offering cleanses us from sin, we Christians are made acceptable to God the Father (Romans 8:1). We then receive, as a gift of faith, the judgment from God that we are sinless like Jesus. We are conferred with Jesus' righteousness through faith. This proclamation allows us access to heaven and perfect peace when our physical bodies die (Romans 5:1-2 and 1 John 2:25). Moreover, and most importantly, we receive the Holy Spirit of God (Acts 2:38 and 1 John 3:34b). We receive the life, the essence of God Himself that empowers us to live according to the spirit and letter of the law. While in this life, we cannot live perfectly. Christians are empowered by the Holy Spirit of God to overcome sin, but we will never be completely free from sinful living in this life.[27] In his letters, Jesus' apostle John writes, "If we (followers of Jesus/Christians) say that we have no sin, we deceive ourselves, and the truth is not in us. If we confess our sins, He is faithful and just to forgive us our sins and to cleanse us from all unrighteousness." (1 John 1:8-9)

It is unfortunate that the law is so often perceived as some sort of dictatorial proclamation made by a heavy-handed God. He is often believed to be the angry, disapproving judge that must be appeased at the cost of one's autonomy and freedom of choice. The fact is, God's command to follow the law is an invitation to a love relationship with Him. Jesus said, "If you love Me, keep My commandments… He who has My commandments and keeps them, it is he who loves Me. And he who loves Me will be loved by My Father, and I will love him and manifest Myself to him." (John 14:15, 21) Again in John 15:10-13, "If you keep My commandments, you will abide in My love, just as I have kept my Father's commandments and abide in His love. *These things I have spoken to you that My joy may remain in you, and that your joy may be full.* This is My commandment, that you love one another as I have loved you. Greater love has no one than this, than to lay down one's life for his friends." Remember, the new covenant that Jesus established was that the law (the 10 Commandments, the ability to love God and each other) would be written on our hearts. "By this My Father is glorified, that you bear much fruit [love well]; so you will be My disciples" (John 15:8).

[Jesus says,] These things I have spoken to you that My joy may remain in you, and that your joy may be full (John 15:11). Accept Jesus' sacrifice, receive His Spirit and get His commandments written on your heart, live in joy. Simple. Not easy because of the lie that we are better off having our own kingdoms and having it our own way. But simple.

Food for Thought

I've heard several people say that they have seen so much hypocrisy in church that they don't want anything to do with church or Christians. I agree that it is unfortunate that people who are a part of a Christian community derive their status and/or self-esteem based on how "holy" they are. The lie is that how well you can perform the show of being a "good Christian" determines your self-worth and your worth in the community. Author Terry Wardle describes it in terms of coming to the table. In the world in order to be invited to sit at the table of preference one must have an education, money, power, position, beauty, etc. However, to be accepted at the Lord's table all you must do is show up admitting your need for a savior. The true Christian recognizes that all knowledge, provision, authority, and beauty come from Him. A person's value and acceptability starts with who He is, not who the person has made him/herself to be. The problem is that the table of the world has made its way into the church. I would like to see churches look more like an Alcoholics Anonymous meeting. People would introduce themselves by saying, "Hello, my name is ____________. I'm a sinner and I need help."

I've heard it said recently that in the great cosmic/spiritual battle for creation, we are both the pawns and the prize. Pawns, because we are players in the battle. We can choose which side we're on. One side is led by a person who is described as love, Father, Creator, all knowing, all powerful, good, to name a few descriptors. The other side is led by a person described as the father of lies, intent on killing us, and destroying all of creation and all that is good. We are the prize, because depending on who we want to believe and align ourselves with we become the one whom they win.

Conclusion

Being at peace spiritually is the beginning of perfect peace. It is simple: Love God, love each other. However, the battle for our eternal essence is the fiercest one ever fought. It took the God/Man Jesus to live a perfect life and sacrifice it for us to make it even possible. To be assured that you are on the right side of this battle, it takes repentance and God's gift of faith and grace. Surrendering to the Prince of Peace is the beginning of perfect peace in every aspect of our lives.

NOTES

[1]David Fiorazo, *Radical Takedown of America: Has the Left Won?* https://www.standupforthetruth.com/2017/03/radical-take-down-of-america/, May 4, 2022.

[2]Dallas Willard, *Renovation of the Heart*, NavPress, Colorado Springs, CO, 2002, page 212.

[3]Nicene Creed, 325 A.D. This creed was first formulated at the First Ecumenical Council, held at Nicea, located in what is now Turkey, in 325, as a response to the Arian heresy, which denied the divinity of Christ. It was revised at the Second Ecumenical Council, held at Constantinople in 381 as a response to the Macedonian or Pneumatomachian heresy, which denied the divinity of the Holy Spirit.

NICENE CREED:

We believe in one God, the Father, the Almighty, maker of heaven and earth, of all that is, seen and unseen. We believe in one Lord, Jesus Christ, the only Son of God, eternally begotten of the Father, God from God, Light from Light, true God from true God, begotten, not made, of one Being with the Father. Through him all things were made. For us and for our salvation he came down from heaven: by the power of the Holy Spirit he became incarnate from the Virgin Mary, and was made man. For our sake he was crucified under Pontius Pilate; he suffered death and was buried. On the third day he rose again in accordance with the Scriptures; he ascended into heaven and is seated at the right hand of the Father. He will come again in glory to judge the living and the dead, and his kingdom will have no end. We believe in the Holy Spirit, the Lord, the giver of life, who proceeds from the Father. With the Father and the Son he is worshiped and glorified. He has spoken through the Prophets. We believe in one holy catholic [universal, Christian] and apostolic Church. We acknowledge one baptism for the forgiveness of sins. We look for the resurrection of the dead, and the life of the world to come. Amen.

[4]In the New Testament, Matthew 5:17-20 Jesus says, "[17]Do not think that I came to destroy the Law or the prophets. I did not come to destroy but to fulfill. [18]For assuredly, I say to you, till heaven and earth pass away, one joy or one tittle will by no means pass from the law till all is fulfilled. [19]Whoever therefore breaks one of the least of these commandments, and teaches men so, shall be called least in the kingdom of heaven; but whoever does and teaches them, he shall be called great in the kingdom of heaven. [20] For I say to you, that unless your righteousness exceeds the righteousness of the scribes and Pharisees, you will by no means enter the kingdom of heaven."

[5]See https://www.sundaysoftware.com/ten/number.htm

for a simple explanation of the differences.

[6]Timothy Keller with Sam Shammas & John Lin. *Gospel in Life Study Guide subtitle Grace Changes Everything.* 2010, Zondervan, Grand Rapics, MI, page 43.

[7]Dallas Willard, *Renovation of the Heart*, NavPress, Colorado Springs, CO, 2002, p. 107.

[8]Martin Luther, *A Treatise on Good Works* (Whitefish, Mon: Kessinger, 1520), Part X18.

[9]Dr. Tim Clinton and Dr. Joshua Straub. *God and Attachment.* Howard Books, A Division of Simon & Schuster, Inc., NY, NY, 2010, p. 16.

[10]Jack Crabtree, http://msc.gutenberg.edu/2001/02/understanding-the-second-commandment/. March 21, 2022.

[11]John Wesley, Commentary on the 10 Commandments, http://www.the-ten-commandments.org/ten-commandments-john-wesley.htm)

[12]James Strong, *Strong's Exhaustive Concordance of the Bible, Hebrew and Chaldee Dictionary,* Abingdon Press, 42nd Ed., 1983, #7722 & #7723, p. 113.

[13]Ibid., #8034, p. 117.

[14]Thomas Watson https://biblehub.com/library/watson/the_ten_commandments/2_4_the_fourth_commandment.htm, March 21, 2022

[15]Larry Wilson, https://wake-up.org/sabbath/saturday-vs-sunday-comparison.html, Aug 23, 2019.

[16]Thomas Watson: https://biblehub.com/library/watson/the_ten_commandments/2_4_the_fourth_commandment.htm March 21, 2022

[17]American society today is a good example of denying God. Forcing Him out of the public square and political discourse has knocked the foundations out from under our freedoms. By denying that our Bill of Rights is based on rights that are inherently given by God we shift moral authority into the hands of humans, who, because of our brokenness, are incapable of keeping morality on the right track.

[18]James Strong, *Strong's Exhaustive Concordance of the Bible, Hebrew and Chaldee*

Dictionary, Abingdon Press, 42nd Ed., 1983, #3513, p. 54.

[19]Is it any wonder that the powers trying to destroy our American culture attack the family and try to separate children from parents?

[20]James Strong, *Strong's Exhaustive Concordance of the Bible, Hebrew and Chaldee Dictionary*, Abingdon Press, 42nd Ed., 1983, #7523, p. 110.

[21]The New Oxford Annotated Bible NRSV footnote for Exodus 20:13.

[22]James Strong, *Strong's Exhaustive Concordance of the Bible, Greek Dictionary of the New Testament*, Abingdon Press, 42nd Ed., 1983, #3710, 3709, p. 52.

[23]One of my pet peeves is when I'm watching a movie and someone watching it with me, who has seen it before, says something like, "This next part is really scarey/funny/sad/_____!"

[24]James Strong, *Strong's Exhaustive Concordance of the Bible, Hebrew and Chaldee Dictionary*, Abingdon Press, 42nd Ed., 1983, #5003, p. 73.

[25]James Strong, *Strong's Exhaustive Concordance of the Bible, Greek Dictionary of the New Testament*, Abingdon Press, 42nd Ed., 1983, page 64.

[26]*Merriam-Websters New Collegiate Dictionary, Tenth Edition*, Fredrick C. Mish, Ed. in Chief, Merriam-Webster, Inc., Springfield, MA, 2000, page 267.

[27]Most of us have heard it said that we are all children of God. Well, according to God's word, the Judeo/Christian Bible, that isn't true. We are certainly all creatures of God, but only those with His Holy Spirit are His children (John 1:12-13).

PART 2

Soul

Mind, Will, and Emotions

Peace is relational, not circumstantial.

GRAHAM COOKE

Introduction

WE ALL RECOGNIZE that some of us are more mentally and/or emotionally healthy than others. Healthy people's minds, wills and emotions are in a condition that allows them to better cope with life. These people seem to have the ability to enjoy life, to live in the present moment in peace instead of regretting the past or worrying over the future. Listed below are a few hallmarks of a healthy soul.

Resilience: This is the ability to bounce back from adversity and to handle stress.

Balance: Knowing that there is a time for everything such as: time spent with people and time spent alone, work and play, sleep and wakefulness, rest and exercise, time spent indoors and time spent outdoors (it is possible to have a nature deficit).

Flexibility: Being able to adapt to situations gracefully without compromising deeply held values versus stubbornly holding to rigid opinions and dogmas. Flexibility involves being in tune to a range of emotions and knowing how to express them appropriately.

Self-actualization: This is living the life God intended for you when He saw you before the foundations of the world were laid. No one does this perfectly. Being aware of and developing your gifts and talents is essential in helping you fulfill your role in creation.

Ability to form healthy relationships: This is perhaps the most important aspect of good mental health. Albert Ellis, one of the fathers of psychology, went so far as to say that good mental health IS healthy relationships. In his book *Prophetic Wisdom*, Graham Cooke says, "Peace is relational, not circumstantial."[1]

How do you form healthy relationships? In my years of counseling and in life I have found that three things are all you need to do to develop healthy relationships and good mental health. They are:

1. Be nice.

2. Think happy thoughts.

3. Mind your own business.

Following these adages does not come naturally. Some of us have personality types that make it easier or come from cultures that resulted in less wounding. Except for the grace and healing power of Jesus Christ, we are hopeless. We can learn better coping mechanisms, train our brains better, bury the pain deeper; but aside from Jesus there is no real avenue for peace and healing. It is Jesus who is the Truth that can dispel the lies and bring peace to our souls and healing to the wounds.

In Part 2: Soul, I will discuss my three rules for good soul care and consequently good relationships. I will offer professional insight from my training and experience as a professional counselor, practical steps to make them part of your life, and biblical support that will feed your spirit and, I hope, give you strength and insight to walk in the grace necessary for your mind, will and emotions to engage in healthy relationship with God and others.

NOTES

[1]Graham Cooke, *Prophetic Wisdom*. Brilliant Book House, Vacaville, CA, 2010, p. 14.

CHAPTER 2

Adage 1: Be Nice

HOW WELL DO you love?

Being nice can mean different things to different people. I once met a man whose father would devolve into a rage and beat him whenever they were beginning to connect as father and son. The father wanted to connect with the son on an emotional level—love him, if you will. The problem was that the father's only experience of male-to-male connection was the rage and violence of his own father. I also know people whose testimony of life is that they never doubted the love and tender affection of their parents. It is no surprise that people from such different backgrounds have very different experiences and expectations regarding relationships.

Our families of origin lay deep foundations for spiritual, emotional, and mental development. The man mentioned above couldn't understand why he had such problems with anger, especially with people he loved the most. The messages conveyed to us in early childhood through our parents' behavior toward each other, toward other people, and especially toward us as individuals, establish a belief system that shapes our individual way of doing the business of life and love. There is a line in the television series "Downton Abbey" where Shrimpy says, "Love is like French or riding: you don't really get the trick of it if you don't learn it when you are young." The ability to love oneself, and therefore others, is shaped by a myriad of things; chief among them is how you were treated as a child.

The perception of oneself in one's environment is key to mental and emotional well-being. It is my opinion that at the root of most, if not all, mental, emotional and spiritual disorder is self-hatred. There are, of course, physical and chemical issues that can contribute to mental/emotional problems. However, if the physical issues are not recognized, accepted and dealt with properly, a belief system that is founded on self-hatred will invade the spirit (a person's essence and driving force) and poison every aspect of life.

It is imperative that we take an honest look at our belief system regarding "love". How does it line up with Jesus' definition: that one lay down one's life for another (John 15:13)? Ask yourself these questions:

- How did my father treat my mother?
- How did my mother treat my father?
- How did they treat me?
- How did other significant people (siblings, teachers, friends, etc.) in my life treat me?
- Does the way I treat others reflect how I was treated?
- Does the way I treat others imitate Jesus in deed AND in thoughts? Am I loving, peaceful, patient, good, kind, gentle, faithful? Do I have self-control?

Answering these questions is not an exercise to discover how well or badly you were treated or how kind or rotten your family and friends were/are. The questions are about discovering how their treatment has affected you and shaped your belief system about yourself, which in turn impacts your behavior. If your perception about yourself is anything other than you are a wonderful creation of a supreme being that understands you, accepts you (not necessarily your behavior), and loves you just because you are His, then you have some work to do regarding your belief system and maybe how you treat people. [See Reactive Cycle Fear Dance, Appendix 2, for a tool to help you sort out your beliefs/emotions and reactions.]

Social Mores — Cultural Expectations

Cultures can be as large as a continent or as small as a family or a couple. A friend of mine has a pillow in his office that says, "I know I live in my own little world, but everybody here knows me." What it means to "be nice" can vary from culture to culture. Look around you. What are the expectations (spoken and unspoken rules) in your community and the culture within it? Does your behavior fit within the structure of the community you live in? If not, are you willing to change in order to fit the community? Or are you willing to take the brunt of other people's rejection because they are uncomfortable with your choice of behavior? Behavior includes: dress (modesty, style, appropriateness to the event), language (words, intonation, or silence), actions (body language, attentiveness, consideration), how you transact business, and social customs.

There are healthy cultures and unhealthy cultures. By healthy culture, I mean a community that is doing its best to love God and love each other according to biblical principles and the grace of Jesus Christ. A good way to judge if your community is healthy is to compare its behavior to the nine fruits of the Holy Spirit found in the New Testament in Paul's letter to the Galatians 5:22 (love, joy, peace, patience, goodness, kindness, gentleness, faithfulness, self-control) or look around and see if your core longings (your need for love, safety, significance, purpose, understanding and belonging) are being attended to and met. (See Chapter 3 for more on core longings.)

If the core longings are not being attended to, chances are the culture is detrimental to emotional, physical and/or spiritual health. If the community you surround yourself with is healthy and you are not, are you willing to make the effort to change? Or vice versa: if your community is unhealthy and you desire to be a healthy individual, are you willing to face confrontation, or even rejection, by a community that insists on staying dysfunctional? In either scenario it may be necessary to disengage from the community/culture by moving away, finding a new set of friends, or even leaving a family for the chance to have your own core longings met and to be a source of meeting them in others.

To be truly healthy, a culture must look like the Kingdom of God. What is the culture of the Kingdom of God? Well, the books that answer that question could fill libraries and it still wouldn't be enough room. It is up to each of us to study scripture and theology for ourselves. In my first theology class my 70-year-old professor said that we each need to determine our own theology. I was shocked at the time. Wasn't I taking the class to learn good theology??!!! Over the years I have found that God is so multifaceted that we can't know everything about Him. He has a particular way that we each as individuals are designed to represent Him, which involves our response to who we see Him as. The lenses through which we see Him are shaped and colored by our families, our communities, the media, our environment, and a host of other things. That is not to say that there aren't certain foundational creeds that hold true across the board (e.g., the Nicene Creed[1]). But our individual experience of Him varies from person to person. He is an absolute entity, but we each have our own perception of Him. The big question is: are we ready to give up our own expectations that are formed by our environment and experiences, and come under the submission of the Kingdom of God, where God is King, and His throne is our heart? The goal of every culture must be to display the attributes of God in every aspect of our lives as we love Him and other people. Only then will there be peace.

MANNERS: basic structures that help us to live with each other.

Most people don't like chaos. For the most part, people feel safer if they know what to expect from people and circumstances. Acting according to the manners expected of you in your community/culture is a way of showing respect to others. It's a way of communicating to them that you value them. It also makes you a safe person to be around. If people don't have to be on guard regarding your behavior, they have time and emotional energy to get to know you at a deeper level, and they more readily open up the deeper places of their hearts to you. Observing and even studying the manners of the culture you are involved with may be worth your time.[2] Remember what Emily Post says:

Manners are a sensitive awareness of the feelings of others. If you have that awareness, you have good manners, no matter which fork you use.

Listed below are a few general manners you may find helpful. For some people many or most of these will seem obvious. For other people, some of them may even seem silly.

General Manners.

- Saying please and thank you
- Not intentionally embarrassing another
- Not talking only about oneself
- Not gossiping
- Not prying by asking intrusive personal questions
- Not asking personal questions
- Not staring
- Not pointing at someone
- Dressing appropriately
- Not talking loudly

Greeting Manners

- Smile.
- Repeat the person's name when introduced to you.
- Remember their name!
- Ask, "How are you?"
- Answer your questions with positivity.
- Respect boundaries especially if it is a first time meeting.[3]
- Say, "Nice to meet you," or "Lovely meeting you."

Dining Manners

- Sit with good posture.
- Lay the napkin on your lap.
- Start eating only when the host has started.
- If there is no obvious 'host', wait for everyone else before you start eating.
- Keep your mouth closed when chewing.
- Take small bites.
- Eat quietly.
- Say, "Excuse me," when you have to use the restroom.
- Keep your area clean and tidy.
- No double dipping unless you are dining with a culture where all the dishes are shared.

Miscellaneous Manners

- Sit and walk straight. Maintain good posture at all times.
- Laugh, smile, giggle, and cry with dignity. Do not make a scene.
- Do not slap your knees, jerk forward or roar with your mouth wide open when you laugh or bawl loudly at the sidewalk when you are sad.
- Try to make as little noise as possible in all situations (when you eat, walk, talk, sit, run, etc.). No slurping, chewing noisily, crunching, e.g. cracking knuckles.
- **Mobile Phone Etiquette:** Do not be occupied with your phone when with people.
- Smile. Be interested in the surroundings.
- It is generally rude to call attention to yourself. (E.g. being underdressed, being overdressed, looking sloppy, etc.)
- Speak properly. Studying your surroundings may be in order here.
- Make it a habit to pronounce your words correctly and use correct grammar. Refrain from mumbling or speaking too fast. Avoid slang, calling people by their pet names or short forms unless you are close to them. Speak as grammatically correctly as you can.
- Never assume anything about anyone.
  "She's so rich, it'll be okay if I don't pay her back for lunch."
  "He's the guy, I should not offer to pay for parking."
  "Someone will surely give you a lift home."
- Ask before touching another person's things, person, or children; or wait until you have been invited to.

- To be on the safe side, never talk about money. "How much does it cost?" "What did you pay for your house?" "How much do you earn?" "How much do you make from your business?" "What is your commission like?"

Simply put, manners are kindness birthed from a loving and considerate heart.

COMMUNICATING LOVE — How attuned are you?

Individuals receive love in different ways. For someone to experience you as a nice person, it is necessary to communicate your love in the language that the person understands. In the big picture, meeting cultural expectations communicates love. In more intimate relationships like families and especially marriage, knowing the love language of those close to you will help in your communication of love and respect. (You can find a test to determine your love language(s) at https://www.5lovelanguages.com/profile/).

Gary Chapman's 5 love languages include the following:

1. Acts of service
2. Physical touch
3. Gifts
4. Quality time
5. Words of affirmation

For example: Mary's primary love language is acts of service. Harry, Mary's husband, feels the most loved through touch. Harry routinely showers Mary with hugs and kisses. Harry would get further with communicating his love to Mary if he would fix the dripping faucet in the kitchen. On the other hand, Mary doesn't understand why Harry gets so upset when she pushes him away while she's trying to get dinner on the table. Both are trying to show love in their own language; unfortunately, the other person doesn't understand the language. It's like talking in English to someone who only understands French. Both Mary and Harry hurt the other by rejecting the other's love that was offered. Sometimes loving someone looks like accepting the intentions of the other person's heart even if it doesn't feel like love in the moment. It's sort of like a kiss from a toddler who has peanut butter and jelly smeared all over his/her face when you're dressed for a special occasion.

As noted above, some people have difficulty receiving love. My experience as a child was that I was dismissed, marginalized and not valued. My reaction was to be submissive at home, but aggressive and arrogant with children my age. I reacted to others from a deep sense of shame that showed itself as anger and pride. As a result, I had difficulty believing people loved me. It is still challenging for me to receive love when it's offered. When I realized as an adult what was going on, I resolved to receive love without waiting for the "feelings" to accompany it. I learned how to simply be thankful and allow my heart to be massaged by the evidence of love. I have also made it a life command to live as Jesus is described in 1 John 4:19 and love first. Knowing that I have difficulty experiencing love, I don't have the luxury of waiting to see if someone loves me before I love him/her. Love first. By loving first, we invite the Spirit of God, who is Love, into whatever situation we find ourselves.[3]

There have been times in my life when it became apparent that I had no power over my self-defense mechanisms, two of which presented themselves as criticalness and aloofness. The culture of criticism and analysis that permeated my family of origin, coupled with my interpretation of it when it was directed toward me (my belief: I was unlovable and unworthy and therefore full of self-hatred) left me with a hard heart indeed. This attitude and these beliefs were ingrained and had been part of my family culture for generations—a part of my DNA, if you will. I had learned a "dialect" that communicated criticism and disdain. My prayer of desperation was for God to give me a new heart that would speak with lovingkindness.

I believe He has done that. After all, because I have by faith accepted the atoning sacrifice of Jesus for myself and received His Holy Spirit, the power over sin that Jesus won through the resurrection is available to me. Since asking for a new heart, I have developed strong aversion to negativity about people and circumstances. It helps me keep my mouth shut. If anything negative does slip into my mind or out of my mouth, if the dialect of my family of origin pops out, I am quick to point out positive aspects of the situation. The evidence is that I am often told how sweet and kind I am.

When my mother was nearly 90 years old and in her last weeks of life, I went to visit her in the hospital. My training in counselling had taught me that one of the best avenues of conversation with elderly people is to talk about their past. So, I asked my mom what it was like growing up. She said when she was six she was standing on the rack wagon and the horses got spooked and ran away with her. Her dad chased the horses down and saved her. And then she said, "You know, mom never spent much time with us kids. She was always busy with the garden or canning or taking care of the house. I never really knew how to do it [love]." My grandmother didn't know how to nurture/love and therefore couldn't teach my mother. It was only a few weeks after my conversation with my mother that my daughter said to me as she was hanging up the phone, "Thanks for loving me so much, mom."

This story of my grandmother, mother, me and my daughter is an example of the transforming power of the Holy Spirit that can break generations of sin. It is obvious that my part in the transformation was minimal. All I did was ask and submit to the promptings in my mind and emotions (e.g., keep your mouth shut, look for the positive, and value what there is to value in the moment). I know my body language and voice inflections are still being pruned to convey unconditional love, and I still have a bit of difficulty believing it when someone tells me I am loving or have a big heart, but I know that my belief system is changing and what I believe in I will grow to be like.

It can be a scary thing to love first. We make ourselves vulnerable to feelings of rejection and even failure. 1 John 4:18 says "There is no fear in love; but perfect love casts out fear, because fear involves torment. But he who fears has not been made perfect in love." The word "torment" is the Greek word *kolasis*, which means penal infliction or punishment.[4] What John is saying here is that we don't love because we fear being punished or even shamed. As we accept the perfect love of Jesus through faith and experience it through encounters with Him and through others, the fear diminishes. Jesus' love is deep, complete and unconditional. It is this love that compelled Him to die for us while we were His enemies. By accepting Jesus' love sacrifice and its removal of the source of guilt and shame (sin, wrong behavior, sense of worthlessness), the roots of fear are removed and we are able to love.

It is my experience that as I intentionally accept the love of others, my heart changes, which makes it possible for me to naturally accept the love of others and in turn love better. It is imperative that we love others. Not only is it the second greatest command according to Jesus, it is what creates peace in society at large. It is foolishness not to be kind, caring and accepting. To do otherwise only causes hurt, which exacerbates our human tendencies to try to gain control through force, which usually manifests in some level of violence or cruelty. A good question to ask yourself when you are feeling defensive is "What am I defending?". Honor? Truth? Pride? (Again, check out the Reactive Cycle Fear Dance tool in Appendix 2).

EMPATHY

In its simplest form, empathy is understanding, which is just as important to our emotional well-being as love. Empathy is being able to feel and relate to the emotional and intellectual state and needs of another person. Most people have an innate ability to sense if another person is genuinely interested in him/her. Even if your body language and your physical attentiveness (eye contact and physical reactions) are indicative of concern, if your heart isn't tuned in, the other person often can tell. True attentiveness communicates, "You're worth my time." Sometimes it is hard to be genuinely concerned about another person. If you have your body language in place, you will at least be less likely to offend them.

Some fundamental physical things that communicate empathy include:

1. *Eye contact*: Look a person in the eye. If you look away, it can communicate disinterest or seem as though the person you're speaking with is not important, or that you wish you were somewhere else besides with them. Eye contact that is intense and unbroken can communicate intimidation or aggression. Your heart attitude toward the person will speak the loudest.

2. *Facial expressions*: A face that reflects the facial expressions and/or emotions of the person speaking will communicate empathy the best. On the flip side, insincerity in your expression could be interpreted as mocking. Again, your heart attitude toward the person will speak the loudest.

3. *Good listening skills*. By simply repeating what a person says to you, the person will feel heard and understood. A good listener's job is to make sure the person speaking knows that you understand them. It is important that you put your agenda aside and focus on the content and meaning of what the speaker is saying. Asking open-ended questions and expressing your interpretation of the speaker's emotions will help the speaker feel understood. If your mind is spinning ahead to formulate a rebuttal, a criticism, or a response in general to what the speaker is saying, you have lost the gift of being present and any real connection is forfeited as well.

NOTES

[1]See note 3 of Chapter 1 for the text of the Nicene Creed.

[2]http://www.elegantwoman.org/manners-today.html, June 4, 2015.

[3]One consequence of not being able to receive love is a propensity to be offended or feel rejected.

[4]James Strong, *Strong's Exhaustive Concordance of the Bible, Greek Dictionary of the New Testament*, Abingdon Press, 42nd Ed., 1983 , #2851, page 43.

CHAPTER 3

Core Longings

Train up a child in the way he should go, and when he is old he will not depart from it.

PROVERBS 22:6

CORE LONGINGS ARE things we need in order to develop and live in a sense of *shalom* and/or complete well-being. Core longings described by Dr. Anne Halley, include love, safety, significance, purpose, understanding, and belonging. People need these core longings to be met from the minute they are conceived. A part of being nice is being a source of these longings for the people around you. Family members, especially parents, have a particularly powerful position in the development of the emotional make-up of children. The natural tendency of small creatures is to depend on the parent or caregiver to provide basic needs. How the core longings are met or not met provides the building blocks of the little person's foundations for emotional development—their belief system. The familiar Proverb 22:6 quoted above applies to negative and positive behaviors.

At early stages in development, experiences shape our beliefs, which can affect our emotional make-up and belief system.[1] A simplistic illustration of how our brain works regarding emotional memory and belief includes the amagydala, the hippocampus, and the prefrontal cortex (PFC), all part of the limbic system. The amygdala is important in the generation of emotions. The information from the amagydala is transferred to the hippocampus, which is instrumental in organizing the information and storing it in the PCF as memory. The amygdala is fully formed and operational at birth. However, the hippocampus is not fully developed until age two or three, when a person learns how to talk. Any emotions experienced during the first two to three years of life can be unprocessed and remain in the person's present emotional state for the person's entire life. For example, a toddler sees her parents fight. Her mother is badly injured and the father leaves. The implicit (subconscious) belief created is that conflict is bad and men are dangerous. This belief could sabotage the little girl's relationships with men until the trauma is processed in order for the emotions to be put in the past as memory, and the perception of herself and the man in the memory is changed to include a sense of safety. This trauma could also paralyze the hippocampus or compromise its development, making any future emotional regulation for the little girl difficult. An effective way of processing the wound is through directed imagery or Christian inner healing prayer. The structure of this type of healing looks like this:

Wound > Lie > Emotional Upheaval > Dysfunctional Behavior (sin) > False Self.[2]

Whenever a core longing is not met, a wound occurs. Since we are in the business of creating homeostasis (peace) for ourselves, in order to make sense of the wound, we will believe some lie about ourselves, the people around us, our circumstances, etc. The wound plus the lie throws us into a state of emotional upheaval (e.g., anger, hatred, depression, anxiety). Again, because we are striving to be at peace, we develop some behavior to relieve the pain. Regardless of whether the behavior is socially acceptable or not, it is dysfunctional if it addresses only the pain of the situation and not the core issues, specifically the lies causing the pain (see Reactive Fear Dance, Appendix 2). In healing prayer, the wound is revisited and Jesus is invited into the memory to bring His perfect interpretation of the situation and His presence (truth) and peace.[3] I have witnessed countless times where the negative belief-creating experiences were overridden through the experience of a loving God and truth as the person revisits the memory where the wound occurred.

On the flip side of this illustration, experiences where the core longings are consistently met create a sense of well-being and confidence in the world, other people, and self. By being an avenue for God to meet the core longings in those around us, we help create peace in the hearts of those in our community and by extension society at large. Whenever we hurt someone, it can come back on us in the form of the negative consequences of the wounded person's dysfunctional behavior toward us or the environment we share. In light of core longings and our role in the lives of people around us, following Jesus' mandate to love one another is only logical. To do otherwise is, quite frankly, stupid.

Definitions of Core Longings:

1. *Love* — My favorite definition of love is "a willingness to value and to avoid devaluing people that springs from a caring, other-focused heart" from Everett L. Worthington Jr., *Hope-Focused Marriage Counseling.*[4] Notice there are three parts to the definition: 1) value, 2) not devalue, 3) a heart that is caring and other-focused. The caring heart values another person in thought, word and deed—don't even think ill of someone, let alone speak negatively to or about them, or act unloving toward them. I've already talked quite a bit about love. And since libraries could be filled with information and philosophies regarding the subjcct, I'll just refer you to the previous pages.

2. *Safety* — This is the condition of knowing you are taken care of, protected, free from harm. Anxiety, the antithesis of peace, stems from some sort of fear and/or feeling unsafe on some level. Feelings of fear can be unconscious or conscious. Beliefs created in our formative years may not connect to a particular person or situation, because the experience that created the beliefs happened before we could process them cognitively. A person who experiences an automobile accident, for example, may have a fear of driving or riding in cars. The accident caused such intense fear (trauma) in the moment that the hippocampus was paralyzed and couldn't process the danger at the time. As a result, the fear of the moment is still present with the accident survi-

vor. The paralyzed hippocampus could not move the emotion to the prefrontal cortex, where the emotional makeup of the person experiences it as in the past.[5]

Being a safe person means others do not feel the need to hide or feel shame in your presence. They know that with you, their needs are important and will be respected and understood if not met. When people are with you, they know they don't have to do anything to feel at peace. In a safe person's presence others know they will not be abandoned, forgotten, hurt, or used.

Being a safe person can help with anxiety in other people, but the fear people experience belongs to them. It's their responsibility to own it and find the help they need. As outsiders, we can only do so much toward helping others feel at peace. (See Chapter 4 about minding your own business.) In the end, it is the inner workings of the person that must be addressed. (See Reactive Cycle Fear Dance tool in Appendix 2.)

3. *Understanding* — Somebody "gets" you. Understanding is not merely cognitive affirmation of a person. When a person feels understood he/she feels attuned to. That is, the other person is present with them and feels their emotions. Their words are heard, comprehended and accepted. Anne Halley describes understanding as "... the empathic joining of my feelings by another who does not judge, resent, reject or discount as I learn, talk, ask for and become." As indicated in the above discussion regarding empathy, being an understanding person is not a passive position in a relationship.

4. *Significance* — You matter. Webster defines significance as "the quality of being important"[6]. If love and understanding are in operation, significance is likely to be at work as well. Significance in its truest foundational form comes from God. No matter what we look like, where we live, who we know, or what we know, we matter because we are part of God's creation. And God is intentional about every detail of His masterpiece. Everything that exists matters, but because humans are made in the image of God, we matter the most. He really does

have all of the hairs on our heads counted. By creating each of the seven-plus billion of us in a unique way, we are all significant. Remember, as part of creation, we all have our own special way that we have been intentionally created for showing off who Jesus is.

This can be a little daunting to grasp. What kind of creature can be aware of all that? Well, for one, God is not a "creature". He wasn't created. He's the Creator. He's been around forever and then some. Part of the problem of grasping this goes back to our propensity to believe that God = ourselves x (fill in the blank)^{n}. Remember, God is not in the equation. He is God. He is other.

It becomes a problem when we look to people or things instead of God to determine our significance. Things and people can change. If we are depending on them to determine our significance and they change, it can throw us into a crisis of identity. It also becomes a problem when our own significance becomes the most important thing. Everything in creation has its own significance. We can waste a lot of time and energy by comparing ourselves to each other in hopes of determining our significance. God sees us and loves us for who we are, not for who we are not. He doesn't want me to be anyone other than Lenore, because Lenore is the only one who can display Jesus' attributes in the particular way I was created to show them off. Being Lenore is enough. I don't have to be anyone else. Part of being nice is acknowledging the significance of yourself and everyone else, and accepting people for who we are, not denigrating ourselves and others for who we are not.

God knows you and sees you before creation in your perfect state. He knows who He created you to be (Psalm 139: 13-17). He has provided a way through Jesus to clean you up from all the muck of sin and death and give you this new, perfect, immortal life. Through all of it, His complete, deep unconditional love for you never changes or diminishes (Romans 8:38-39).

5. *Purpose* — You contribute to your community. You have a job. There is a goal you have a part in. In Chapter 4 of this book I'll talk

about minding your own business, that is, knowing and establishing good boundaries and being content in who you are. For now, know that each one of us has a specific purpose established for us because of our design. "My gifts and talents are part of my design in being made in the image of God. My purpose is not informed by or found in what I am good at or what I can do for this world, others or God." (Anne Halley) My design is informed by my purpose. The main purpose is to as perfectly as possible display the reputation and character of the One through whom everything (including ourselves) was created—Jesus. Because of who we are, we operate in this world in a particular way and take up space that has been assigned to us. Our behavior and position is heavily influenced by a myriad of things including culture, environment, personal physical attributes. It is not always obvious or easy to know what our job is either in the moment or in the long run, career-wise or in relationships. In those times of uncertainty, follow the basic tenets of what it means to be nice according to the customs and culture you find yourself in as it is filtered through biblical principles. You can always fall back on the golden rule of treating others as you want to be treated. Or "What would Jesus do?"

Knowing what Jesus would do is accomplished through studying the Bible, reading the Bible for inspiration through meditation, spending time with other people who are filled with God's Holy Spirit, spending time in prayer, reading books on Christian living. (Richard Foster's *Celebration of Discipline: The Path to Spiritual Growth* is a wonderful book explaining Christian spiritual disciplines.) Remember that as a believer, you are under the grace of God. He will direct your path. As Oswald Chambers says, "Trust God and do the next thing" (*My Utmost for His Highest*, devotional for February 18). I'm not convinced that there is a hard and fast "right or wrong" about decisions we make, if our hearts are truly desirous of doing God's will. God is not either/or, but both/and. He promises to be with you "until the end of the age" (Matthew 28:20). He promises to direct your path (Proverbs 3:5-6). He also promises to use all things for your good (Romans 8:28). That doesn't mean that He thinks all things are good, but that He will *use* them for your good regardless of how the enemy means to harm you. In other words, follow your heart boldly knowing that the Holy Spirit lives in it, God's laws are written upon it, Jesus' blood covers it, and God's grace abounds toward it. As you allow Him to clean you up (i.e., sanctify you), you will more and more perfectly represent Him in the manner you were created to represent Him in creation.

6. *Belonging* - you are part of something–no matter what. Halley describes belonging as "...my felt place of being with, rooted, welcomed, joined without any feeling of loss or fear." There are a whole myriad of ways we can "belong": country, species, ethnicity, family, religion, political affiliation, sex, philosophy, emotional attachment, social class, economic standing, language, neighborhood, and the list goes on. Our individual DNA is the foundational building block of the physical body and will never change. For instance, every human on earth has genes that identify or inform the cells in the body that this body is a human. Research has proven that all humans come from the same ancestral parents (Adam and Eve, if you will). As a result, regardless of race, ethnicity or where a human lives, they can join with another healthy human of the opposite sex from any other race, ethnicity or country and the offspring will be human and able to reproduce. Who your biological family is will never change as long as you live. DNA is DNA. Your family has a powerful position at the switch of how your genes are expressed.[7] Family can also be a social group of people committed to each other and attached emotionally and mentally.

I grew up in a large Roman Catholic family, whose history of Roman Catholicism dates back at least 400 years and possibly to the time of Constantine. (Constantine is actually our direct ancestor.) My family has a strong sense of identity and culture that is attached to this religion. At one point in my journey, a Protestant piano tuner named Paul shared the Gospel of Jesus with me in a way that opened my eyes to see that relationship with Jesus and His saving grace is more important than the religion of a set of rules and rituals. When Paul left, my piano was tuned to play the right notes, and my heart was tuned to Jesus. I knew I had to leave the Catholic Church to follow

Jesus in this new way. And if I left the Catholic Church, I would have to leave my family. I sat down on my couch and cried for two hours straight. I loved my family and the Church with all its beautiful liturgy and structure. I was grieving the deep sense of belonging I gained from both.

My family has a lot of European blood. We all have fair skin and blue or blue/green eyes. For most of my life we assumed that our surname, Jarboe, was French. However, during his extensive research on our family tree, my brother Mike discovered that there are people in Iraq with surnames that are very similar to ours. After further research, my brother found that the first Jarboe in America could have been educated by French monks who were known to take boys from the Middle East and educate them in France. Moreover, one of my nephews discovered a whole community of Iraqi immigrants near him whose last names are several variations of Jarboe. The Iraqi community can trace their Christian heritage back to the first century when the apostle Thomas converted their family to Christianity.

It was a bit of a paradigm shift to change my sense of identity and belonging from being Western European to Middle Eastern. As an American, so much of the history I was taught, which naturally gave me a sense of identity and belonging, had a heavy European influence, with very little about the Middle East. As a result of the new historical evidence, there is a niggling in a deep place in my heart that I'm not who I thought I was and that I don't belong to my country the way I thought I did. It's a somewhat irrational thought. My dad's family has been in North America since 1635 and helped settle the United States, and my mother's family is Western European. Nonetheless, there are a few members of the family who won't accept the Iraqi evidence.

Attachment Styles

How you attach—how you know others and how you let yourself be known—strongly affects your sense of identity (your perception of how you fit into community) and vice versa. Does your sense of self influence your attachment style, or does your attachment style determine your sense of self? The answer is probably "both/and" rather than "either/or." Attachment styles can be inherited through personality or culture. Again, genes can be "turned on" (epigenetics) when circumstances are right. Attachment style is a window into how you perceive belonging and how you let yourself be known. Curt Thompson, MD, in his book *Anatomy of the Soul* makes this comment:

> ...it is only when we are known that we are positioned to become conduits of love. And it is love that transforms our minds, makes forgiveness possible, and weaves a community of disparate people into the tapestry of God's family.[8]

Attachment is a foundation stone for moral behavior (how you love God and love others) and is a strong factor in how you live in community. For more about attachment, see Appendix 1.)

Of the three adages (be nice, think happy thoughts, mind your own business) being nice is the most important. The apostle Paul in his letter to the Corinthians (1 Cor. 13:13) says that love is the greatest virtue. Without love, everything else—all our attempts at doing life well—are pretense and noise. When we love, we look like our heavenly Father, who is love.

NOTES

[1]Dr. Tim Clinton and Dr. Joshua Straub, *God Attachment: Why you believe, act, and feel the way you do about God.* Howard Books, A div. of Simon and Schuster, Inc., Ny, NY, 2010, page 57.

[2]Terry Wardle, *Healing Care Healing Prayer.* New Leaf Books, Orange, CA 2001 pages 127-144.

[3]In the New Testament book of John, chapter 14:6 Jesus refers to Himself as "the way, the truth, and the life".

[4]Everett L. Worthington Jr., *Hope-Focused Marriage Counseling*, InterVarsity Press, Downers Grove, IL, 1999, page 33.

[5]There are several effective treatments for trauma including: EMDR (eye movement desensitization and reprocessing), directed imagery and/or inner healing prayer, Theosphostic prayer, to name a few. If you suffer from obsessing over an event, reliving a trauma, or experiencing undue anxiety, you may want to consider getting help from a trained trauma specialist. There may be an experience in your past that cognitively seems pretty harmless. However, your belief system (either conscious/ explicit or unconscious/implicit) may still be compromised in such a way that leaves you in a state of anxiety. Experiencing the peace of the presence of a safe person can help calm anxious people, but processing the initial point of trauma is essential for sustained relief.

[6](*Merriam-Webster's Collegiate Dictionary, 10th Ed.*, Merriam-Webster, Inc., Springfield, MA, pg. 1088).

[7]Epigenetics is a process by which genes are turned off and on. This doesn't change the DNA genome, but it can change how the DNA is expressed.

[8]Curt Thompson, *Anatomy of the Soul.* Tindale Momentum, Tindale House Publishers, Inc, Carol Stream, Illinois, 2010, page 3.

CHAPTER 4

Adage 2: Think Happy Thoughts

belief + thoughts + emotion = behavior

or

emotions + thoughts + behavior = belief (system)

?

REGARDING THE IMPACT emotions and thought processes have on our lives, there are two trains of thought: one says our thoughts control our emotions; the other says that our emotions control our thoughts. It's probably both. During life before age two our rational cognition is recorded as emotion and affects our belief system implicitly and for life if it isn't proven otherwise through experience. Therefore, the foundations of our beliefs and consequently our behaviors are established in emotional experience. Emotion controls thought, or at least it affects it. As we develop, cognitive interpretation begins to have more of a role in the development of our thought patterns and belief system.

An individual does not live out of her knowledge, she lives out of her belief system. Our belief system is the sum of all one's emotions, empirical knowledge, thoughts, imaginations, body reactions, and experiences. My experience personally and as a licensed professional counselor leads me to believe that experience affects belief systems the most profoundly. We spend a lot of time and energy, consciously and unconsciously, looking for facts and opinions (knowledge) that agree with our belief systems. We do this because what we believe creates the emotional reality we live in and our template for homeostasis. It is a scary thing to have one's reality threatened. It threatens the things we rely on to keep us at peace: culture, our sense of self, our moral bearings, finances, home, etc. Changing one's belief system takes some courage—and pain.

People will not change if change is more painful than keeping the status quo. Pain comes in many forms: physical, moral conviction, loyalty, religious guidelines, cultural expectations, fear of rejection, etc. In the final analysis, the question is how much pain are you willing to endure in order to live in peace, and what does that "peace" involve? Obviously, if what is most important to you is your physical well-being, you wouldn't be willing to die for it, preferring to capitulate to anything that threatens your physical comfort. Dying would only make sense if you were convinced that by doing so you would be transported into another "life" or a higher state of being. People are also willing to die for a "cause" or ideal when they see themselves as a part of an entity (e.g. nation, family, religion, ideology, or political movement) that they value more than their individual existence. Ben Franklin, a great proponent of individual freedom, said "Those who would give up essential Liberty, to purchase a little temporary Safety, deserve neither Liberty nor Safety."

The problem is that our world is broken by sin and so are our perceptions. There is a popular meme that refers to "my truth." If all of your perceptions and analyses are factual, then I suppose you live in "truth." However, every perception is shaded by logic that is not based on all the information in existence and/or an interpretation of information that is skewed by brokenness. Absolute truth must come from outside of creation from a Source that knows all the facts and their nuances and is morally perfect and unaffected. Only a holy Creator/God can do that. Thus Jesus calls Himself the Way, the TRUTH and the Life. He came from outside of creation as the one through whom all creation came into existence (He knows all the facts including those outside the realm of human perception) to model perfection in thought, word and deed by living a sinless life.

For by Him all things were created that are in heaven and that are on earth, visible and invisible, whether thrones or dominions or principalities or powers. All things were created through Him and for Him. And He is before all things, and in Him all things consist. Colossians 1:16-17

By calling our belief system our "truth," we relegate absolute truth to the dustbin of modern relativism, thus elevating ourselves and our belief system to the position of God. Our belief system is perhaps what is real to us, but not necessarily truth in a broader eternal sense.

If you look for truth, you may find comfort in the end; if you look for comfort you will not get neither comfort or truth only soft soap and wishful thinking to begin, and in the end, despair. C. S. Lewis

By thinking happy thoughts, "renewing the mind", we can clear up our perception of reality so that it agrees with Truth/Jesus, the Prince of Peace, thus making it possible to live in perfect peace (*shabat shalom*).

Retraining your brain (creating new neural pathways) is not an easy task. It takes intentionality and some humility. Admitting that you have faulty thought patterns may be the hardest step in gaining a mind that rests in peace. If you are a person that derives self-esteem from being "right", giving up your opinions about the comparative "wrongness" of people, circumstances, ideas, etc., may threaten your sense of self worth and your feelings of superiority, which may be providing a sense of safety. If you are comparing yourself to or focusing on anything or anyone other than your Creator for your sense of self, it is idolatry and rooted in pride.[1] If you dig deep, you will find that any pride you have is likely rooted in shame, especially pride that points the finger in ridicule or condemnation towards others or yourself. Pride alleviates deep feelings of unworthiness or worthlessness, which is shame.

I'm not talking about being analytical. Some people who have wonderful analytical minds are humble people. The line between analysis and criticalness is a matter of the heart. Remember, humility is knowing who you are in Christ and who He is in you and living that without apology (my definition). When your assessment crosses over into the realm of condemnation, you have entered the court of right and wrong or good and bad, and you are the judge. You're probably the jury, the prosecuting attorney and the executioner as well. Check your attitude. Analysis looks at the circumstances and answers with a loving invitation, "This is the way, walk in it." Criticism and judgment look at the person and say, "You are accused, guilty, condemned and abandoned." Destructive criticism and judgment deny the value and purpose of people and life. Only God has the wisdom for eternal condemnation and abandonment of a person.

Your job in renewing the mind is to focus on "whatever things are true, whatever things are noble, whatever things are just, whatever things are pure, whatever things are lovely, whatever things are of good report, if there is any virtue and if there is anything praiseworthy—think on these things" (Philippians 4:8).

This is no easy task. Most of the world and most of our culture and media in the U.S. are saturated with messages that do not agree with the Bible, which must be our source for renewal.

That's a pretty strong statement. What about all the other philosophers and thinkers in history? Admittedly, the statement comes from my belief system—my knowledge plus experience—which has affected how I operate in the world, which has reinforced my belief system. The thing that the Bible and the Christian belief system have that others don't, is the influence of the Holy Spirit of God, Creator of heaven and earth and all that is seen and unseen.

I grew up in a "Christian" home that was deeply culturally Roman Catholic. I was devoted to living my life according to the teachings of the church and following God in that religious system. There came a time in my life when I became hungry for a deeper experience of God.

That hunger led me to surrender my life to Jesus Christ and accept Him as my only hope for redemption and the avenue for deeper relationship with God. As I did that, I became filled with Jesus' Spirit, "born again" in evangelical terms. From that moment, the Bible read like a different book. The stories and teaching became food for my soul and spirit. You see, the author of the Bible is the Holy Spirit of God. He used hundreds of people through the ages to pen the thoughts of His heart toward those who are or have the potential to become His sons and daughters. The Spirit moving through those writers was the same Person living and moving in me to point out what I needed to see and hear. It's the same today, almost 40 years later. The same passages I have already read dozens of times in my life often take on new meaning and substance, because the Spirit in me knows me and what I need at each particular time of my life to encourage me, comfort me, give me wisdom and essentially grow me into a more perfect image of Jesus.

If our highest purpose for life is to represent Jesus in the earth, then using the ultimate source that explains His thoughts and ways, the Bible, only makes sense. There are dozens of translations available. If you are sincerely seeking God and a peaceful way of living, I believe He will lead you to the translation that is right for you and your particular journey with Him.

Begin with the Gospel of John in the New Testament (NT). That book talks about the love of Christ for us. Then read through the NT at least three times before you attempt to read the Old Testament (OT). In the OT, reading the Psalms and Proverbs daily is a good way to wash your soul with wisdom and understanding for life and godliness. Having the biblical foundation will help you to know what is right thinking. Remember the 10 Commandments in Chapter 1 and use them as guardrails for life decisions, attitude adjustments and trains of thought. Especially remember the two commands that Jesus says are the greatest: love God above everything else, and love your neighbor as yourself.[2]

At one point in my life, my thoughts often (2-3 times per day at least) engaged in sexual daydreaming. I knew this to be impure and sinful and that the thoughts displeased God. I also came to realize that my mental and spiritual health depended on changing these patterns. Instead of fighting against the thoughts directly ("I'm not going to thinking about that!"), I turned my thoughts to Jesus, confessed the sin, asked forgiveness and help, and then started talking to Him about whatever was present—the weather, my plans for the day, His love for me, my love for Him, whatever. It took awhile (years in fact), but I can honestly say that now I rarely have those types of thoughts. And when I do, I apologize to Jesus and immediately turn my thoughts to Him.

[The Lord] will keep him in perfect peace, whose mind is stayed on thee... (Isaiah 26:3).

Your worst enemy cannot harm you as much as your own unguarded thoughts. Buddha[2]

Another place to look for healthy ways of thinking is in science. Any type of self-help book or information explaining the human soul can be helpful if it is based on biblical principles. If you're looking for truth through science, you will find God. He created everything. In his book *Feeling Good*, David Burns, a psychologist, lists 10 ways of unhealthy thinking he calls cognitive distortions.[3] If any of these ways of thinking sound familiar to your way of thinking, consider a healthy alternative.

1. All-or-nothing thinking: You see things in black and white categories. If your performance falls short of perfect, you see yourself as a *total* failure.

2. Over-generalization: You see a single negative event as a never-ending pattern of defeat.

3. Mental filter: You pick out a single negative detail and dwell on it exclusively so that your vision of all reality becomes darkened, like a drop of ink that discolors the entire beaker of water.

4. Disqualifying the positive: You reject positive experiences by insisting they "don't count" for some reason or other. You maintain a negative belief that is contradicted by your everyday experiences.

5. Jumping to conclusions: You make a negative interpretation even though there are no definite facts that convincingly support your conclusion.

- **Mind reading:** You arbitrarily conclude that someone is reacting negatively to you and don't bother to check it out.
- **The Fortune Teller Error:** You anticipate that things will turn out badly and feel convinced that your prediction is an already-established fact.

6. Magnification (catastrophizing) or minimization: You exaggerate the importance of things (such as your goof-up or someone else's achievement), or you inappropriately shrink things until they appear tiny (your own desirable qualities or the other person's imperfections).

7. Emotional reasoning: You assume that your negative emotions necessarily reflect the way things really are: "I feel it, therefore it must be true."

8. Should statements: You try to motivate yourself with shoulds and shouldn'ts, as if you had to be whipped and punished before you could be expected to do anything. "Musts" and oughts" are also offenders. The emotional consequence is guilt. When you direct should statements toward others, you feel anger, frustration, and resentment.

9. Labeling and mislabeling: This is an extreme form of over-generalization. Instead of describing your error, you attach a negative label to yourself: "I'm a loser." When someone else's behavior rubs you the wrong way, you attach a negative label to him: "He's an idiot." Mislabeling involves describing an event with language that is highly colored and emotionally loaded.

10. Personalization: You see yourself as the cause of some negative external event for which, in fact, you were not primarily responsible.

When you find yourself being triggered negatively by something or someone, check your thoughts against the above list. It may be helpful to consult with a trusted friend or counselor; they may see something, good or bad, about your thought process that you don't. Take some time to separate yourself from the situation emotionally, and look at yourself and the situation as objectively as possible. Another powerful tool is the Reactive Cycle Fear Dance exercise (see Appendix 2). This exercise will help you determine the roots of negative thoughts and feelings and the wrong beliefs you have been allowing to rule your life.

When my older granddaughter was three years old we were sitting at her little table working on a project. I was scrunched into her little chair with my knees poking above the tabletop. I don't remember what we were doing, but we were making a mess. I made some comment about the mess we were making to which my little granddaughter replied, "That's okay, we're just learning." Remember, it takes time to renew your mind, to learn new habits of thinking and ways of believing. A big part of the process is learning to have grace and patience with yourself and those around you.

"The things which you learned and received and heard and saw in me, these do, and the God of peace will be with you." Philippians 4:9

Henry Bodkin says, "...research show[s] that negative thoughts can be physiologically harmful, while positive thinking calms the heart rate and even boosts the immune system." Bodkin goes on to say that while lack of criticism or neutrality is helpful to the psyche, compassion toward oneself is what results in positive bodily responses including lower heart rate and decreased sweat response.[4] It's no wonder that my own mother, who was given to criticism and shame, suffered from high blood pressure and stroke. The negativity she espoused was likely directed toward herself as much or more than those around her.

"...out of the abundance of the heart the mouth speaks. A good man out of the good treasure of his heart brings forth good things, and an evil man out of the evil treasure brings forth evil things." Matthew 12:34-35

Mindfulness

Mindfulness practice can potentially develop a comparably reassuring internal presence by offering us (glimpsed or sustained) experiences of *the selfless, or universal, self that is simply awareness*. Such experiences are often marked by profound feelings of security, acceptance, and connection in relation as much to others as to ourselves.[5] (Emphasis mine.)

Learning to control or be intentional about our thoughts takes some practice. One aspect of maturity is learning to think before you speak. We all have life scripts that are "talking" to us all the time. If our formative years have included caregivers and associates who provided positive affirmation and genuine love and care, the voices in our heads will likely provide healthy influence to our well-being. Appendix 3 is a list of affirmations that we need to hear for positive living. How does the list compare to what you have heard or are still hearing from the influential people in your life? Go through the list. Mark the affirmations that you did not hear in your developmental years. Hearing them and making them part of your thought processes will be helpful in bringing wholeness to your overall well-being and sense of self. Write the marked affirmations on note cards and speak them out loud to yourself. Try taking them one at a time and for a week speak an affirmation over yourself and live like you believe it. Take some time to think about what it means to have permission to think in a new way about yourself and your world. When I meet with couples, I often have them give their cards to each other and speak the affirmations to each other.

Other mindfulness exercises include the following:

Deep breathing: Take deep, slow, intentional breaths in through the nose and out through the mouth. Pay attention to how the air feels cool coming in and warm going out. As you take deep breaths from your diaphragm, the diaphragm actually massages the spinal cord.

Being mindful of your surroundings: When you find your mind wandering during an activity, bring your thoughts and intentions into the present moment by being mindful of your senses (touch, smell, hearing, sight) and how they are responding in the moment.

Remember, *shalom* is a state of well-being that includes every part of our being. Not only will our minds be at peace, but our bodies as well.

NOTES

[1]Pride: when your expectation about yourself or anyone else is different from God's. Pete Kuiper 2014: personal communication.

[2]Suman Jyoty Bhanta, *Buddha's Real Teachings,* "Quotes on Buddha Teachings." https://buddhasrealteaching.wordpress.com/2012/01/22/quotes-on-buddha-teachings/ (cited May 11, 2022).

[3]David D. Burns, M.D., *Feeling Good:The New Mood Therapy*. Avon Books, Inc., New Your, NY 1980, pages 32-41.

[4]https://www.telegraph.co.uk/science/2019/02/07/think-no-evil-kind-thoughts-can-boost-immune-system-study-finds/ . Published, February 7, 2010. Cited, March 30, 2022.

[5]David J. Wallin, *Attachment in Psychology*. The Guilford Press, New York, NY, 2007, page 6. Wallin cites Linda Grahm's 2006 personal communication.

CHAPTER 5

Adage 3: Mind Your Own Business

"If it is possible, as much as depends on you, live peaceably with all men."

ROMANS 12:18

IN ORDER TO mind your own business, it is necessary to know what *your* business is. And in order to know what your business is, you need to have an idea of who you are and where you fit into your part of the world—who and what are you responsible *for*, and who and what are you accountable *to*.

Boundaries

A boundary is a defining factor that everything in creation has on some level. It is something that determines where one thing ends and another thing begins. Walls, fences, property lines, city limits, county lines, etc., all indicate where one area ends and another begins. Another example is our skin. Our skin determines where our body begins and ends. Even unseen things such as emotions, mental acuity, cultural expectations, and spirituality have limits that give definition to the person possessing them.

It may help you have a better sense of self and autonomy if you take a look at and verbalize who you are in terms of the space you take up physically, mentally, emotionally, culturally and spiritually. As humans we need to be connected to other humans. Sometimes those connections get fuzzy and your individual uniqueness gets diminished or even lost altogether. God has designed each of us uniquely for a unique purpose: to positively display some attribute of Him in a particular way. How we have been created has precious value to the Creator. Only I can present Jesus in the way He has created me to represent Him.

So then, what are my boundaries? The skin or epidermal layer of our bodies is probably the most obvious personal boundary. It determines what space our physical vehicle occupies in space. We have a right, or have been given permission to take up space, simply because God created us and we are part of His plan. Determining just exactly where that actual physical space is can be a challenge.

The first place is your mother's womb. Because you're alive, and because your mother has been selected by God to be your mother, she is mandated by Him to provide the unique pre-birth environment that is the launch pad for the rest of your existence. Some scientific advances such as *in vitro* fertilization, surrogate mothers, transplants and genetic engineering have complicated the definition of "mother" and "womb" where persons begin their lives. Nonetheless, the new human has unique surface structure of cell membranes, then cells, and finally skin as the body develops. Wherever that happens, this new creation is unique and human, designed in the image of God.

When babies are first born, they do not have a sense of autonomy. In their minds, they are one with their mother; that is, their sense of self is not separate from who their mother is. Separation from the natural mother in the earliest stages of development can be profoundly traumatic. The child's innate sense of self can be disrupted, causing anxiety or confusion as his/her anchor for existence is disturbed. While in the womb, the child can hear the mother's heartbeat, her voice and the voices and other sounds around the mother. The infant can sense the emotions of the mother and develop his/her sense of what the world is and how he/she needs to be in it to survive. Even in the womb the child can create defense mechanisms—walls if you will—for survival, or at least the perception of survival. (For more discussion, see Appendix 1: Attachment.)

As you get older your sphere of influence broadens, as do the resources available to shape you in a way that best displays your eternal essence. The small child does not have the wherewithal to possess much responsibility or accountability to his/her world. When he is very small, he doesn't have much to bring to the table except potential and his humanity. As she grows she learns what is acceptable and what is not acceptable in terms of behavior, priorities and goals for life. In a healthy environment the child is respected as a person regardless of the level of development of any skills or intellectual abilities or contributions she may be capable of bringing to the table.

Until you develop a mature sense of eternal purpose, survival is the most pressing need. Survival involves all kinds of needs. Let's go back to core longings: love, safety, significance, purpose, understanding and belonging. These are the things that we will consciously or unconsciously strive for at every level of existence. How we perceive our level of fulfillment regarding each of them will determine how we develop our boundaries.

As I have stated earlier, we live in a world that is ruined by sin and consequently we are all wounded in some way. Consciously or unconsciously, we tend these wounds every minute of our lives, struggling against the pain and the lies we have come to believe in order to make sense of our world. In our struggle to survive, we develop behaviors and ways of thinking that protect us from the pain and unease. Unfortunately, these barriers not only shield us from pain, but they divide us from other people. This makes relationships with other people challenging at best and sometimes impossible.

The following illustration depicts two people in relationship. The lines around the persons represent defense mechanisms. For the most part relationships are just the defense mechanisms bumping up against each other.

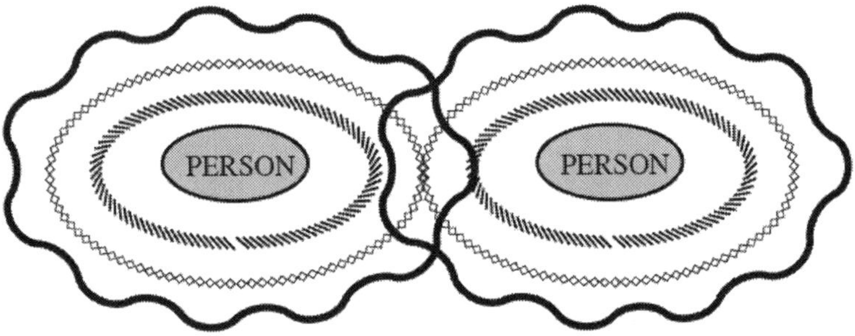

In an ideal world, we would be safe enough with each other that we wouldn't feel the need for defense mechanisms. We long for intimacy, to be known and loved for who we are and to know and love others for who they are. More often than not, defense mechanisms mask who we really are. People who are good at relationship are free to be themselves and to let others be themselves as well. They know the difference between a healthy boundary and a wall that attempts to hide weakness. They are full of grace for themselves and for others.

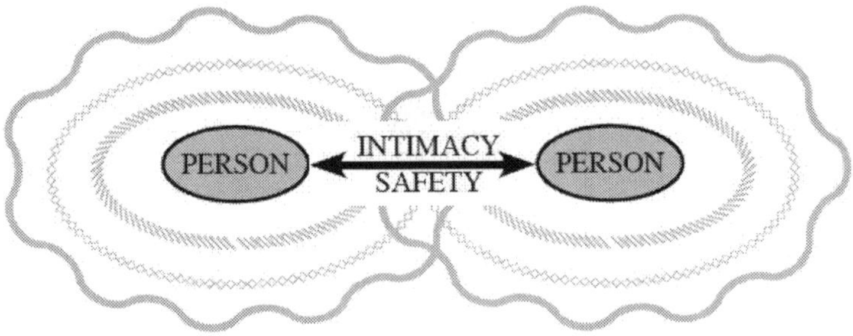

Except for the grace and healing power of Jesus Christ, we are hopeless. We can learn to establish boundaries and better coping mechanisms, train our brains better, bury the pain deeper, but aside from Jesus there is no real, lasting avenue for peace and healing. It is Jesus Who is the Truth that can dispel the lies and bring peace to our souls and healing to the wounds.

I highly recommend the classic book, *Boundaries*, by Dr. Henry Cloud and Dr. John Townsend[1]. The book is a wonderful resource for learning about boundaries and how to begin establishing healthy boundaries. For now, I want to touch on two important aspects of boundaries Cloud and Townsend cover in depth: the laws of boundaries, and the myths involved with boundaries. The laws are Cloud and Townsend's ideas, the comments in each section are mine unless otherwise noted.

The 10 Laws of Boundaries[2]

1. *The Law of Sowing and Reaping:* Your actions, thoughts and attitudes have consequences. This isn't a threat by God or civil authority that you need to "do it my way, OR ELSE". It is simply the way of creation. We were created with a mind and will of our own, and God respects that. He gives us the freedom to make our own choices largely because He doesn't want our love to be coerced. (Remember John 14:15, "If you love Me, you will obey My commands.")

2. *The Law of Responsibility*: Your life is your own. There is a right of passage into maturity that is marked by the realization that it is your responsibility to do something with the life you have been given and then embracing that responsibility with faith, hope and love. Cloud and Townsend say, "...anytime you are not loving others, you are not taking full responsibility for yourself; you have disowned your heart. We are to love one another, not be one another. You are responsible for yourself. I am responsible for myself (Phil. 2:12-12)."[3] A deeper level of maturity begins when we stop pointing the finger at people and circumstances and turn our finger toward our self first, acknowledging our part (both positive and negative), and then turning our hand toward God for help and strength for the life He reveals to us. It very likely will involve repentance and forgiveness toward ourselves, others and circumstances. (See Appendix 4: Forgiveness.) It will take a new revelation of self, which results in a new revelation of God, and/or vice versa *ad nauseum*.

3. *The Law of Power*: You can change/affect some things, and not others. The first sentence in the Serenity Prayer reads: "God, grant me the serenity to accept the things I cannot change, the courage to change the things I can, and the wisdom to know the difference..." (Attributed to Reinhold Neibuhr, 1892-1971). Even in serenity or passivity a person decides whether or not they will act. Not making a decision is essentially making a decision to not decide. There is power exerted. In each of the parts of the Serenity Prayer, a decision to act is made. The fact that you are reading this book is proof that you are no longer immobilized. Granted, in the case of trauma and being frozen from fear, the brain/body literally shuts down. There are three particular lies that are routinely embedded in a belief system when a person experiences trauma: you have no voice, you are alone, you have no power. These three lies strike at the core of personhood.[4] These lies are a direct attack on your humanity and the image of God that you are. If you have trouble making decisions or if you procrastinate or feel "stuck," you may need to need help exploring how the lie of powerlessness may be affecting you.

4. *The Law of Respect*: It is important to respect others' boundaries and yours. It is very honoring to let someone make decisions for his/her own life and feel the consequences of those decisions, good or bad. When you don't protect your own boundaries you are essentially abdicating your personhood to the rule of someone else. You are giving up your individual humanity, just like a country that doesn't protect its boundaries loses its unique culture and identity. This is a bit of a balancing act. We need to be part of community, which involves compromise and give and take. However, if we find we're giving more than we're getting from a relationship, it's time to step away and reevaluate the situation. Is the relationship helping me to grow into a stronger, more loving version of my true self, or am I being used? Am I able to use my voice? Do I feel empowered? Do I feel like I am accepted unconditionally for who I am?

5. *The Law of Motivation*: Why do you keep or not keep boundaries? If you are having trouble creating boundaries (standing up for yourself), consider this: are you backing down because of love or

because of fear? You may fear loss of love or abandonment, others' anger, loneliness, losing the "good me" inside, guilt, burden to pay back emotional or relational debt (i.e., duty, approval, over-identification with the others' loss). "If you serve to get free of your fear, you are doomed to failure."[5] For more discussion on love vs. fear motivation in relationship, please see Appendix 5.

6. *The Law of Evaluation*: Hurt ≠ Harm. In the process of establishing healthy boundaries, relationships will likely feel some tension. If you come from an unhealthy situation regarding boundaries, everyone involved will likely feel off-balance when one person starts behaving differently by setting healthy boundaries. A lot of feelings will likely be hurt, including your own. Feelings of rejection and abandonment may be expected on both sides. The big question for you is: is it worth it? For example, in Mary's family (fictitious) there is the unspoken rule: "If Momma ain't happy, nobody's happy." In this example Momma has to have her way or she creates a situation so uncomfortable that everyone gives in. Momma has trained the people of her domain well. When Mary finally stands up to Momma, Mary is verbally attacked, humiliated and told to leave and not come back until she's ready to do what Momma wants. Mary has a choice. Does she succumb to Momma and stay in the comfort of familiarity even though it is toxic and damaging? Mary would do well to consider what core longings are being met in Momma's domain: love (is she valued and not devalued), safety (is she at peace), significance (do her needs and desires matter), purpose (is she free to grow into the person God has created her to be), understanding (is she seen, heard and accepted for who she is), belonging (is she embraced and celebrated as an individual part of the community). Momma has overextended her boundaries in a way that violates Mary's boundaries and denies her personhood, her humanity. Momma denies the image of God that Mary is. If Mary's family were living in a pool of sewage they would recognize the toxicity and get out. The toxicity of constant tyranny and abuse is no less damaging emotionally and spiritually. If you have a bad splinter, removing it hurts but it doesn't harm you. Allowing the unhealthy situation (the splinter) to remain could cause serious infection and even death.

7. *The Law of Proactivity*: Overcoming victimhood and being assertive. The first stages of establishing boundaries may take some "violence" to overcome the inertia of entrenched habits. By violence I mean expressing pent-up anger, withdrawing from community[6], cutting apron strings. Eventually, you will have to reenter the human race you have reacted to by proactively, assertively expressing yourself and reconnecting on the grounds of mutual love and respect. Romans 12:18 says "If possible, *so far as it depends on you*, be at peace with all people" emphasis mine. Some people don't want to live in a culture of love and respect. If that's the case, you can and should walk away.

8. *The Law of Envy*: Learn to be content. In the journey of discovering your unique way of representing God in creation, it is natural to look around you and see things and situations that you want for yourself. These things can be inspirations that encourage you to take risks, stretch and grow so that you can live in the fullness of who you are created to be. They become a problem when you look at them with resentment and entitlement. It becomes a boundary problem because you are looking outside yourself—the boundaries that determine you—to chase a journey and identity that is not yours, thus violating someone else's boundaries if not openly, in your heart. Each individual is on a journey of fulfillment of his/her created purpose in Jesus. The details of the journey are obscure and take shape through all kinds of opportunities and choices. The only way we can completely miss it is if we deny Jesus in it. If you belong to Jesus, He will use everything (things perceived as good or bad) for your good (Romans 8:28). "Good" is referring primarily to oneness in a love relationship with Him. Secondarily, "good" refers to you letting Him shine through the essence that is you, regardless of the circumstances. Envy and resentment just muddy the vessel (you) that holds the Spirit of Jesus.

9. *The Law of Activity*: I heard a wise man say once that people are only victims of their own ignorance, laziness and bad decisions. In order to create and maintain good boundaries, it is necessary to be vigilant against the forces of evil, who are continually prowling the earth in search for someone to destroy (1 Peter 5:8). Growing in wisdom and knowledge and being an active participant in life are essential in

protecting ourselves. Passivity can become an ally of evil by failing to resist it. God will do His part as Protector, but He expects us to do our part in life as well. He has privileged us with that important role in our lives and His creation. "The sin God rebukes is not trying and failing, but failing to try."[7]

10. *The Law of Exposure*: Let your boundaries be known. By expressing your thoughts, opinions, desires, likes and dislikes, etc., you give definition to yourself. Keeping yourself hidden is a type of manipulation and deception. If the good in you (i.e., the things about your life that line up with scripture and Jesus' teachings) cannot be expressed openly, maybe it's time to find a culture where they can be. If there are things about your personality or behavior that you don't want exposed because they don't line up with scripture and Jesus' teachings, those things need to be confessed and worked out of your life.[8] Being comfortable in your own skin starts with being honest with yourself about who you are and then being honest with those around you.

The bottom line of all these laws of boundaries has to do with living a life of humility. Remember, humility is knowing who you are in Christ and knowing who Christ is in you and living it without apology. Know your boundaries, live within them and make others aware of them. Honor others by respecting their boundaries and letting them experience the consequences of their decisions.

Myths about Boundaries

In Chapter 6 of their book *Boundaries*, Cloud and Townsend list a number of myths that are common misconceptions about boundaries.[9] It's helpful to be aware of these, because believing them may prevent you from establishing or preserving good boundaries. I recommend reading the book for a more in-depth discussion of each.

Myth 1. If I set boundaries, I'm being selfish.

Truth: Appropriate boundaries actually increase our ability to care about others. Poor boundaries result in irresponsibility and mismanagement of resources.

Myth 2. Boundaries are a sign of disobedience.

Truth: If we can't say "no," we can't say "yes." An internal no nullifies an external yes.

Myth 3. If I begin setting boundaries, others will hurt me.

Truth: It is a poor relationship when the self-hatred of one is affirmed by the other's lack of respect. "Boundaries are a litmus test of the quality of our relationships."[10]

Myth 4. If I set boundaries, I will hurt others.

Truth: Boundaries are not a weapon to attack others with, they are a tool to preserve what is truly yours.

Myth 5. Boundaries mean that I am angry.

Truth: The more you exercise your rights to good boundaries, the less anger you will feel. Anger is a secondary emotion. When your boundaries are threatened and you feel angry, what is the emotion driving the anger? (See Appendix 2.) It's beneficial to express the anger in a calm, healthy manner so that good relationship can be established or restored.

Myth 6: When others set boundaries, it injures me.

Truth: Others' boundaries only hurt you if you're too dependent on them. If you get hurt by others' boundaries, maybe it's time to expand your circle of friends (i.e., so you won't be so emotionally dependent on a few people). Maybe it's time to take more direct responsibility for your own affairs (e.g., curtailing your spending habits or getting a second job to cover your expenses instead of borrowing from the friend who turned you down for a loan).

Myth 7: Boundaries cause feelings of guilt.

Truth: Except in business, relationships are not quid pro quo or transactional. Another good reason to be clear about your boundaries is so there are no assumptions as to what the relationship involves. Different cultures have different expectations, (e.g., some cultures expect the next generation to provide for the elders). Unless otherwise clearly spoken, gifts of time, money, attention, love, etc. are given freely without expectation of repayment.

Myth 8: Boundaries are permanent, and I'm afraid of burning my bridges.

Truth: You own your boundaries. They don't own you. Boundaries can be renegotiated as relationships change and mature. For example, if you set a boundary to establish that your time is your own, you can feel safe to spend time with someone as they show that they respect your time.

A Brief Look at Identity

Your identity is made up of hundreds of identifiers: earth dweller, human race, gender/sex, ethnicity, nationality, family, religious belief system, occupation, personality traits, eye color, etc. We also define ourselves in terms of what we believe other people think of us. In the USA one of the first things we ask a stranger is, "What do you do for a living?" The answer can infer all kinds of things: education, socioeconomic status, intellect, power, influence, personality, likes and dislikes, etc. Unfortunately, the answer can also pigeonhole us and even trap us if we are not living out of our true self. Take a few minutes and write down as many things as you can about yourself that describe who you are and your current place in society and your particular community. Then rank them from 1 to 5 in terms of how much they influence your sense of self.

In the middle of writing this book, I moved from Colorado to Texas. In Colorado I was a licensed professional counselor working in a highly respected agency. I lived in a small town where I was known as an educated professional and spiritual leader in my church. When

I moved to Texas, my counseling license didn't transfer; no one knew me as a professional. I was known in my family as mom, mother-in-law and grandma, but because of the nature of my work (counseling) I really couldn't talk about work. The result was that external definitions of who I am were severely pruned. The thing the Lord was calling me to the most strongly was writing, something that was new to me and in the earliest stages of development. Only a few friends and family members were aware of this. Again, if I was looking to people or circumstances to define me and give me a sense of worth, I had to do some major reassessment.

It was not easy. I came to the realization that the Conductor of this symphony that is my life is directing me through a new movement. Some instruments in the orchestra of my life were quieted while others were called on to step forward and be heard. The sounds of the professional, mature Christian have been hushed so the voice of the grandmother and mother of adults could be practiced and tuned. Hidden rumblings of my soul were being asked to make themselves heard in what I write. I was still the same person that the Lord saw before Creation. Circumstances and surroundings continue to train me and influence how that personhood is expressed. I am still learning who I am in Christ and who He is in me. I am still learning to accept His deep, complete, unconditional love that helps me live that identity without fear, and present Him as He has ordained me to, without apology, relying on His infinite grace and mercy and the power of the resurrection.

Ideally, our primary descriptor is beloved child of God. Being convinced of God's love and our own lovability diminishes a whole boatload of fear (1 John 4:18). For the most part, it is the fear of not being loved and accepted (along with the other core longings not being met) that keeps us from living in the peace of our true self. It is in self defense of that fear that a false self takes on identity, obligations and expectations that don't belong to our true self. We end up not minding our own business. Our truest business is to stay focused on the One who created us and knows who we are. By receiving the truth of who we are from Truth Himself (John 14:6)—from the one who calls

Himself love (1 John 4:16)—we fulfill our highest purpose (i.e., complimenting Jesus by expressing in ourselves and with our lives a unique positive attribute of Him). We are not to be more like all of who Jesus is, but more like our true self, which is just one part of His Body.

NOTES

[1]Dr. Henry Cloud & Dr. John Townsend, *Boundaries*, Zondervan, Grand Rapids, MI 49546 2017.

[2]Ibid., pages 93-94.

[3]Dr. Henry Cloud & Dr. John Townsend, *Boundaries Participant's Guide Revised*, Zondervan, Grand Rapids, MI 49546 2017, page 40.

[4]Diane Langberg, *Counseling Survivors of Sexual Abuse*, Tyndale House Publishers, Inc., Wheaton, IL 1997, pg 37.

[5]Dr. Henry Cloud & Dr. John Townsend, *Boundaries*, Zondervan, Grand Rapids, MI 49546 2017, pages 93-94.

[6]Dallas Willard says that because humans are such creatures of community, to withdraw is an act of violence.

[7]Dr. Henry Cloud & Dr. John Townsend, *Boundaries*, Zondervan, Grand Rapids, MI 49546 2017, page 101.

[8]James 5:16 states, "...confess your sins to one another, and pray for one another so that you may be healed." In the context of this passage, James is referring to physical healing. However, according to modern research, much physical disease is due to anxiety and lack of forgiveness. If we live according to our Creator's laws (in this case, honesty) we are promised lives of peace and wholeness. God doesn't promise a comfortable life, but He does promise peace.

[9]Dr. Henry Cloud & Dr. John Townsend, *Boundaries*, Zondervan, Grand Rapids, MI 49546 2017, page 105-122.

[10]Ibid., p. 105.

PART 3

Body

...present your bodies as a living sacrifice to God...

ROMANS 12:1

CHAPTER 6

Keeper of the Presence of God

"...do you not know that your body is the temple of the Holy Spirit..."

I CORINTHIANS 6:19

GENESIS 1:26-28 GIVES an account of the beginning of humanity and its intended foundational structure. The attributes given to humans include dominion over the other creatures, male and female sexes, and the command to multiply and fill the earth. In Genesis 2:7 scripture says, "the Lord God formed man of the dust of the ground, and breathed into his nostrils the breath of life; and man became a living being."

In Psalm 139:14 the Psalmist calls us "fearfully and wonderfully made".[1] Our physical body, as well as the rest of us, is precious. The Psalm tells of God's intentionality toward us, which is an indication of how valuable we are to Him. I've copied the entire psalm below (emphasis mine).

Psalm 139
For the Chief Musician. A Psalm of David.

O LORD, You have searched me and known me.
You know my sitting down and my rising up;
You understand my thought afar off.
You comprehend my path and my lying down,
And are acquainted with all my ways.
For there is not a word on my tongue,
But behold, O LORD, You know it altogether.
You have hedged me behind and before,
And laid Your hand upon me.
Such knowledge is too wonderful for me;
It is high, I cannot attain it.

Where can I go from Your spirit?
Or where can I flee from Your presence?
If I ascend into heaven, You are there;
If I make my bed in hell, behold, You are there.
If I take the wings of the morning,
And dwell in the uttermost parts of the sea
Even there Your hand shall lead me.
And Your right hand shall hold me.
If I say, "Surely the darkness shall fall on me,"
Even the night shall be light about me;
Indeed, the darkness shall not hide from You,
But the night shines as the day;
The darkness and the light are both alike to You.

For You formed my inward parts;
You covered me in my mother's womb.
I will praise You, for I am fearfully and wonderfully made.
Marvelous are Your works,
And that my soul knows very well.
My frame was not hidden from You,
When I was made in secret,
And skillfully wrought in the lowest parts of the earth.

Your eyes saw my substance, being yet unformed.
And in Your book they all were written,
The days fashioned for me,
When as yet there were none of them.
How precious also are Your thoughts to me, O God!
How great is the sum of them!
If I should count them,
They would be more in number than the sand;
When I awake, I am still with You.

Oh, that You would slay the wicked, O God!
Depart from me, therefore, you blood thirsty men.
For they speak against You wickedly;
Your enemies take Your name in vain.
Do I not hate them, O Lord, who hate You?
And do I not loathe those who rise up against You?
I hate them with perfect hatred;
I count them my enemies.
Search me, O God, and know my heart;
Try me, and know my anxieties;
And see if there is any wicked way in me.
And lead me in the way everlasting.

God designed humans to be His temple on earth, the place where His presence dwells. 1 Corinthinans 6:19 says, "Or do you not know that your body is a temple of the Holy Spirit within you..." To get a glimpse of just how precious we are, let's look at two places in the Old Testament where God instructs His people to build a physical place where His presence would be: the Tent of Meeting, or Tabernacle, which the Israelites transported on the journey through the wilderness, and the Temple of Solomon built as a permanent structure in Jerusalem. Both of these structures are forerunners of the final Temple Jesus establishes by His death and resurrection, His church (i.e., individual believers and His corporate "body" at large).

The Tabernacle: Exodus 26-31

The Tabernacle was a large mobile structure that designated a specific location where the Presence of God would be among the Israelites as they traveled through the wilderness on their way from Egypt to the Promised Land. Moses had specific instructions from his face-to-face conversations with God regarding how the Tabernacle was to be made. As you read about it in Exodus Chapters 26-31, you will notice how all the materials were of high quality and costly.[2] And yet, whole structure and its contents were designed so they could be dismantled and put on lowly ox carts and transported through the wilderness.

God designated specific men to build the Tent of Meeting, the Tabernacle and the Ark of the Covenant. He had "filled [these men] with the Spirit of God, in wisdom, in understanding, in knowledge, and in all manner of workmanship" to create the Tent, the Tabernacle and all the utensils (Exodus 31:2-6).

The vestments for the priests were made from specific instructions as well. "You shall make holy garments...for glory and for beauty" (Exodus 28:2). The garments were made with fine linen made of "gold, blue, purple and scarlet thread" (Exodus 28:5). The breastplate was inlaid with precious stones set in gold. Peter writes that believers in Jesus "are a chosen people, a royal priesthood, a holy nation, a people for God's own possession" (1 Peter 2:9). The colors and materials of the priests' vestments indicate how valuable their work is, as well as how valuable the priests are to what God is doing in the earth. They took care of the place of His presence in the Old Testament, and believers in Jesus HAVE BEEN AND ARE the place of His presence since Jesus' crucifixion and resurrection. After Jesus ascended bodily into heaven, as seen by eyewitnesses (Acts 1:9), He sent the Holy Spirit to fill and empower His disciples (see Acts 2).

The primary job of the Tabernacle and Temple was to carry out the rituals for atonement (forgiveness and payment of sin) so that the presence of God would be among them. The beautiful and costly vestments of the Old Testament priests were sprinkled with the blood of a ram (Exodus 29:21) and anointed with oil. Both elements are symbolic of purification and initiation for a specific purpose. A gold plate on the priest's turban was inscribed with the words "Holiness to the Lord" (Exodus 28:36). And so it is for every believer, covered with the forgiveness provided by Jesus' blood. Our most fundamental identifier as humans made in His image and carrying His presence is holy—set apart—to the Lord.

The Temple of Solomon

Solomon was the son of King David. David was responsible for reuniting the tribes of Israel and bringing the Promised Land under the rule of the people of Israel. At one point in his reign, David wanted to build a permanent structure to house the Ark of the Covenant. However, the Lord spoke to him through the prophet Nathan and denied him the honor, because David had been a man of war and had shed much blood (1 Chronicles 28:3). The Lord also told David that it would be his son, Solomon, who would build the Temple. The Lord gave David specific written instructions about the architecture and materials for the building and all the furniture and utensils needed for the rituals to be performed. Furthermore, David collected the gold, silver, bronze, iron, wood, precious stones and marble needed for the construction of it all. (See 1 Chronicles 28:11 through 1 Chronicles 29:9.) Total cost for the gold and silver alone at today's price (February 2022) is about $322,000,000. No expense was spared. The finest materials were used, and the most skilled artisans were employed to do the work. The leaders and the people willingly contributed to the collection of materials for the Temple. (For a detailed description of the temple, see 2 Chronicles chapters 3 through 5.) Then David said,

> "O Lord our God, all this abundance that we have prepared to build You a house for Your holy name is from Your hand, and is all Your own. I know also, my God, that You test the heart and have pleasure in uprightness. As for me, in the uprightness of my heart I have willingly offered all things; and now with joy I have seen Your people, who are present here to offer willingly to you." (1 Chronicles 29:16-17).

The Temple and the Tabernacle were both made of costly materials fashioned by skilled artisans, valuable beyond expression. So too are our bodies, which have been fashioned to hold the Presence of God the Holy Spirit.

The Temple of the New Testament

When Jesus was still walking the earth in bodily form, He made the statement that He would tear down the Temple (his followers were looking at the Temple of Solomon) and in three days build another one (Mark 14:58, John 2:19). Jesus was talking about His physical body. Seventy years later, after the Christian church, the Body of Christ, had been established, the Romans came through Jerusalem and destroyed Solomon's Temple. The gathering place and cultural center for the Jewish religion has not been rebuilt to this day. There are synagogues all over the world, but no Temple. Again, it is God's desire that humans be the place where His presence dwells, where His mercy and splendor are displayed, where His name/character are represented in the world.

Referring to the sacrifices of the Old Testament places of worship, in Romans 12:1 Paul urges the new Christian church to "offer yourselves as a living sacrifice" to God. Peter encourages the body of Christ to

> "...[lay] aside all malice, all deceit, hypocrisy, envy, and all evil speaking, as newborn babes, desire the pure milk of the word, that you may grow thereby, if indeed you have tasted that the Lord is gracious. **Coming to Him as to a living stone, rejected indeed by men but chosen by God and precious, you also, as living stones, are being built up a spiritual house, a holy priesthood, to offer up spiritual sacrifices acceptable to God through Jesus Christ**." 1 Peter 2:1-5 (Emphasis mine.)

What is in the heart of His people has always been preeminent with God. When David was being anointed for kingship over Israel, he was the youngest and smallest of his father's sons. Jesse, David's father, couldn't believe that David would be chosen king. Samuel says, "...God does not see as man sees...but the Lord looks at the heart" (1

Samuel 16:7). In the above passage from 1 Peter, the symbolism refers to a building, but Peter is talking about the heart, the essence of who we are as part of the Body of Jesus.

In Luke 17 Jesus talks about the kingdom of God. In verse 21 he says, "the kingdom of God is in your midst. The Amplified Bible says "among you [because of my presence]". The operative word in the passage is the Greek word *endidoosko*, "to invest with a garment: clothe in, wear".[3] In other words, the kingdom of God is manifested when we are "wearing" Christ. Romans 13:14 says, "put on the Lord Jesus Christ, and make no provision for the flesh in regard to its lusts."

When we put on clothes, we take on a certain appearance. Clothes can indicate culture, socio-economic status, family, preference in taste, morality, religious preference, etc. When we allow all these aspects of our lives to be influenced by the teachings of Jesus and His presence in us, we are recognizable as the kingdom of God. Jesus said, "By this all people will know that you are My disciples [part of my kingdom]: if you have love for one another" (John 13:35). The King of Heaven led by example; He laid down His life in the ultimate sacrifice because He loves us completely. He is love.[4]

Because perfect love dwells in us through Jesus' Holy Spirit, His splendor is displayed more perfectly in humans than any other part of creation. We were created to express more succinctly who He is than the majesty of the mountains, the power of the oceans, the fruitfulness of the plains or the vastness of starry deep space, and better than any other living creature. We can let His love flow through us like no other creature or part of creation. Humans have been ordained for the place of highest honor in creation. We were given responsibility to use the resources the Lord provides to take care of and use honorably our bodies to display Christ and His attributes.

NOTES

[1]There are rumblings in the bioengineering and artificial intelligence worlds suggesting that we may be able to download the contents of our brains/minds into a man-made vehicle that looks very much like a human being. See https://www.rt.com/usa/229811-mind-clones-robot-afterlife/ September 29, 2021. I find it interesting that at the highest levels of artificial intelligence, the robots develop their own language and talk to each other. http://thirdmonk.net/knowledge/robots-create-language-bbc-artifical-intelligence.html September 29, 2021. Their conversations have led to talking about taking over the humans. God made man in His image; perhaps inadvertently, man creates things in his image, too. https://www.treehugger.com/intelligent-robot-reveals-plans-take-over-world-chilling-interview-4862970 September 28, 2021.

[2] https://connectusfund.org/meaning-of-the-11-most-important-colors-in-the-bible October 25, 2021).

[3]*Strong's Concordance, Greek Dictionary of the New Testament,* page 28, #1737.

[4]I sometimes describe the Presence of Jesus as being like perfume. When you spend time with someone who wears perfume, you take on the fragrance. It sort of hovers around you and recreates part of the experience of being with the person wearing it in the first place. When we spend time with Jesus in prayer, talk about Him with other people, and spend time studying the Bible and letting His ways and life soak into our thoughts and habits, we begin to take on the essence of who He is—His fragrance, if you will.

CHAPTER 7

Scripture and Our Physical Bodies

"...God created [humankind] in His own image..."

GENISIS 1:27

Then God said, "Let Us make man in Our image, according to Our likeness'; so God created man in His own image; in the image of God He created him; male and female He created them. Then God blessed them, and God said to them. "Be fruitful and multiply." Genesis 1a; 27-28

And the Lord God formed man of the dust of the ground, and breathed into his nostrils the breath of life; and man became a living being. (Genesis 2:7)

THE FIRST MENTION of humans in scripture is located in the Genesis creation narrative (above). In the beginning God spoke to the earth to bring forth creatures, but "formed" man out of the ground. "Formed" comes from the Hebrew word *yawtsar*, to press through the squeezing into shape; to mould into a form; especially as a potter.[1] "Then God said, 'Let the earth bring forth the living creature according to its kind..." (Genesis 1:24). True to the special relationship He has with humans, God created man through touch and the other creatures by command. God wishes to mould us with personal interaction rather than edict. God is definitely to be revered as LORD and King; however, He also calls us sons and daughters (2 Corinthians 6:18) and even friends (Genesis 18:17, Exodus 33:11, John 15:15).[2]

Moreover, God created the perfect companion for Adam from one of his ribs.

> And the Lord God caused a deep sleep to fall on Adam, and he slept; and He took one of his ribs, and closed up the flesh in its place. The rib which the Lord God had taken from man He made into a woman, and He brought her to the man. [23]And Adam said: "This is now bone of my bones and flesh of my flesh; she shall be called woman, because she was taken out of Man. Therefore a man shall leave his father and mother and be joined to his wife, and they shall become one flesh. (Genesis 3:21-24)

As in all things about life, the essential element is relationship. The Trinity (Father, Son, and Holy Spirit) have been in perfect relationship forever. Their unity is so perfect that they are "one," in thought, purpose, character, power, etc. One. As a result, their relationship is perfect. Since humans are made in God's image, the same type of perfection in relationship is the modality in which we represent God most perfectly, and thus is the goal of our humanity.[3]

Jesus descended out of eternity and became a mortal man in part so He could fully understand the human experience and be a more effective priest or mediatory agent between humans and God.[4] In the same way, Adam, being formed out of creation, had a oneness with it that helped him to understand it and all the creatures in it. As a result, he was better able to wield his dominion with grace. Moreover, the perfect companion for Adam was created from him so that they would have a deeper understanding of each other, so much so, that their union would be referred to as being "one flesh." As I have said before, the union of a man and a woman in covenant relationship and physical intercourse is the most holy act on earth because it most perfectly represents God. When the sexual act is perverted, it is a serious affront to God because it is a serious distortion of His image.

American society is so sexualized that it is a challenge to tease out what sex is according to God's design and what is perversion. Unfortunately, according to scripture, most of what we see on television and the movies and hear about in the media is some kind of perversion. Scripture says that the wages of sin is death (Romans 6:23). And sexual sin can lead to literal death and certainly emotional and spiritual turmoil.

When you live in sin for a long time, it becomes the norm. It becomes a way of life, and you become desensitized to its destructive properties. This is especially true of sexual sin. The sex drive is one of humanity's most powerful drives, the drive to carry on the species and specifically your personal DNA. Once you have engaged in sex, it is very hard to get the genie back in the bottle, so to speak.

Humans are created to release a powerful, euphoria-producing chemical, oxytocin, during orgasm. Research finds that this pro-social hormone contributes to relaxation, trust, and psychological stability. It's no wonder that sex can be a powerful addictive force. When you feel these feelings with another person, it bonds you to the person, satisfying the human longing for connection. In a life-long, monogamous relationship these effects can be helpful in solidifying the union. However, the more partners you have, the less likely you are to bond deeply. Having only one partner for life is God's way of protecting the individuals and the couple as the foundation of a healthy society.

The sexual act between a man and woman is the most sacred in creation. It represents who God is better than any other. As a result, when it is distorted through any type of sex other than between a committed man and woman whose union is sanctioned by their community and covenant, the image of God is distorted more profoundly than by any other sin. Thus, we need to look at what God says about it in the Bible.

Let's start with the New Testament:

> Now the body is not for sexual immorality, but for the Lord, and the Lord for the body. And God both raised up the Lord and will also raise us up by His power. Do you not know that your bodies are members of

> Christ? Shall I then take the members of Christ and make them member of a harlot? Certainly not! Or do you not know that he who is joined to a harlot is one body with her? For "The two," He says, "shall become one flesh." But he who is joined to the Lord is one spirit with Him. Flee sexual immorality. Every sin that a man does is outside the body, but he who commits sexual immorality sins against his own body. Or do you not know that your body is the temple of the Holy Spirit who is in you, whom you have from God, and you are not your own? For you were bought at a price; therefore glorify God in your body and in your spirit, which are God's. 1 Corinthians 6:13b-20

"Sexual immorality" is translated from the Greek word *porneia*: harlotry (including) adultery and incest; idolatry: fornication.[5] Let's look at each one separately.

1. Harlotry: lacking legal or moral restraints regarding sexual activity.[6] The people Paul was writing to used the Old Testament laws for sexuality as their compass for sexual activity.

2. Adultery: voluntary sexual intercourse between a married man or married woman with someone who is not his or her spouse.[7]

3. Incest: sexual intercourse between persons who are closely related.[8] (Just how close is too close is defined in the Old Testament, Leviticus Chapter 18.)

4. Idolatry: "the worship of a physical object as a god: immoderate attachment or devotion to something".[9]

5. Fornication: consensual sex between two people who are not married to each other.[10]

Now let's look at what the Old Testament law has to say about sex. Grant you, there are over 600 laws that the Jewish community had set in place in Jesus' time. They included laws regarding civil, ceremonial, and moral aspects of their culture. The civil and ceremonial laws became obsolete due to Jesus' ultimate sacrifice for sin and the revealed mystery that the Gentiles were to be part of the Kingdom of God, too. The moral laws, including the 10 Commandments, stayed in place. In the New Testament writings when there is controversy about what laws need to remain in place, sexual purity is always mentioned. The players of the time were thinking in terms of what the Talmud had to say about sexual purity; it makes sense to use those laws as guidelines for sex.

See Leviticus Chapter 18. Verses 6 through 18 delineate family relations that are too close for sexual relationships. They include: father, mother, father/mother-in-law, step-father/mother, sibling or half-sibling, step-siblings, grandchildren, aunts/uncles (blood and through marriage), son/daughter-in-law, a person plus his/her child. Verses 22-23 specify the "abominations" of homosexuality (same-sex relations) and bestiality (sex with animals).

Verse 21 of the chapter says, "And you shall not let any of your descendants pass through the fire to Molech, nor shall you profane the name of your God: I am the Lord." Suddenly, and in the midst of the enumeration of sexual perversions, the reader of Chapter 18 is warned against idolatry. Part of the reason why the sexual act is so sacred is because the result under favorable circumstances is new life. Offering the fruit of this holy act as a sacrifice to another deity was forbidden and punishable by exile from the community and from the territory (see vv. 25 and 29). Any type of child neglect, abuse, or even murder (in the case of abortion) is a type of sacrificing the small life for the selfish pleasure or ambitions of the abuser. Verses 23-25 explain that by engaging in the enumerated forbidden sexual acts the people as individuals are defiled (polluted), the nations (people as a group) are defiled, and the land (earth, ground, fields) are corrupted. The gods of convenience, career, sexual appetite, social standing, cultural expectations, etc., are powerful influences, which can harm innocent children and curse their appointed caretakers and the caretakers' means of sustenance. More profoundly, it profanes the name of God, and thus circumvents the purpose of human existence.

New Testament references describing sexual sin include 1 Corinthians 6:9-10. "Neither fornicators, nor idolators, nor adulterers, nor homosexuals, nor sodomites, ... will inherit the Kingdom of God." Again, sex acts outside the covenantal relationship between a man and a woman are enumerated as the means of prohibiting us from entering into the kingdom/culture of God.

Verse 11 continues, "And such ***were*** some of you. But you were washed, but you were sanctified, but you were justified in the name of the Lord Jesus and by the Spirit of our God." (Emphasis mine.) The forgiveness and cleansing power of the blood of Jesus and the life-changing power of the resurrection with which believers in Jesus are infused can help them overcome old habits and ways of living that are detrimental to them, even ways that are rooted in powerful physical and emotional drives such as sex and ambition. Many people belonging to the LGBTQ+ community testify that they were "born that way," that they can't remember being anything else (i.e., having heterosexual attractions). I don't dispute that. I have never experienced those inclinations; therefore, I cannot truly understand the power of them nor the sense of identity they carry. Here some things that I do know:

1. One can live a long, fruitful, satisfying life in celibacy.

2. Temptation is not sin. Giving in to temptation and acting out the sin is when guilt is conferred. Usually, when we become believers and receive the Holy Spirit we have numerous bad habits and ways of thinking that take time to change. Our brains must literally be rewired. As we refuse to travel the old paths, they will grow over and new paths conducive to the principles of the kingdom of God will be paved. While the new ways of life are being established, we must trust in the forgiveness, grace (unmerited favor) and patience of the Lord. He understands the struggle and the power of sin and brokenness. His forgiveness is already yours. He has taken your guilt and shame.

3. In repentance new life is possible by the power of the Holy Spirit. In the two years before I was saved I was embroiled in an adulterous affair. I experienced the power of the lies that said it was okay

because my spouse was absent and negligent. My brokenness and loneliness overrode the strength of my guilt and any moral determination to end the affair. The choice to break it off with this guy was virtually impossible. But when I gave my life to Jesus, all the feelings for the man disappeared. I experienced a deeper more powerful love that cascaded over me in waves and sealed my citizenship in His kingdom. Every experience of repentance is different. The Lord meets each one of us at our specific point of need.

4. You have to decide if following Jesus is worth it. Matthew 5:29-30 says,

> "[29]If your right eye causes you to sin, pluck it out and cast it from you; for it is more profitable for you that one of your members perish, than for you whole body to be cast into hell. [30]And if your right hand causes you to sin, cut it off and cast it from you; for it is more profitable for you that one of your members perish, than for your whole body to be cast into hell."

I don't believe that Jesus meant for you to mutilate your body in order to keep yourself from sinning. Rather I believe He meant that you were to heed its sinful proclivities as though it were not a part of you. Giving up sexual orientation, for example, can mean giving up an empowering sense of identity. It means uprooting a pervasive sense of your existence and planting it in Jesus so that He becomes your primary identifier and source of life. Be assured, sexual sin isn't the only sin that demands a new sense of identity.

5. The decision is not whether or not to engage in behavior that is morally wrong, rather even in the midst of temptation, the decision is whether or not to follow Jesus. Do I or don't I surrender to the kingdom of God and give up kingship of my own kingdom (i.e., give up citizenship of my old culture).

Again, let me emphasize that the verse refers to the sinners in past tense. "And such ***were*** some of you." Change IS possible through the One who rose from the dead.

Your body is your most precious asset. To use it in a manner that is not conducive to its created purpose is not only destructive but foolish. It's not just a physical construction, but it is inhabited by superior intellect, an eternal spirit and life obtained from God having breathed into us. Only human bodies can house God's eternal Spirit and eternal life.

NOTES

[1]James Strong, *Strongs Hebrew and Chaldee Dictionary*, page 61 #3334 & 3335.

[2]It is any wonder that touch is an essential element for human development? During WWII, the Nazis tried to create a pure race by taking newborns from their mothers and raising them without touching them for fear of contaminating them. The babies failed to thrive, and some even died.

[3]Again, the most important thing in life is love (1 Corinthians 13). Jesus said that the greatest commandment is to love God and the second is to love each other. In Jesus' final discourse He commanded us to love one another as He loves us, willing to lay down our lives for each other (John 15:13).

[4]"Seeing then that we have a great High Priest who has passed through the heavens, Jesus the Son of God, let us hold fast our confession. For we do not have a High Priest who cannot sympathize with our weaknesses, but was in all points tempted as we are, yet without sin. Let us therefore come boldly to the throne of grace [*place of relationship*], that we may obtain mercy and find grace to help in time of need. For every high priest taken from among men is appointed for men in things pertaining to God, that he may offer both gifts and sacrifices for sins. He can have compassion on those who are ignorant and going astray, since he himself is also subject to weakness. Because of this he is required as for the people, so also for himself to offer sacrifices for sins" (Hebrews 4:14 to 5:3).

[5]*Strongs Greek Dictionary of the New Testament*, page 59, #4202.

[6]Paraphrased from *Merriam-Webster's Collegiate Dictionary, 10th edition*, page 530.

[7]Ibid., page 17.

[8]Ibid., page 586.

[9]Ibid., page 575.

[10]Ibid., page 459.

Epilogue

IN 2014 I broke my ankle. It happened as I was finishing up a long counseling session with a client. When I went to get up, both of my feet were dead asleep. I tripped over my right foot and landed on my left foot, which was turned sideways. You could hear the pop as I dislocated my ankle and fractured the tibia and fibula. My dear friend and the agency's office manager rushed me to the hospital and stayed with me while I had emergency surgery. My church community circled around me and took care of me 24/7 for the first five days of my convalescence.

After about two weeks of limited mobility, I was sitting on my couch with my ankle propped up on a stack of pillows. I had come to realize that I needed to be more involved with my community and was ready to do that. I was talking to the Lord and said, "Okay, Lord, I'm sorry for being too independent. Will you please just heal me so I can get on with life?" It was then that the word "defiant" came into my mind. Whoa. That was a level independence I didn't realize I had reached.

God showed me that as His creation and especially the Body of Christ (those people filled with His Spirit), we are representatives of who He is in creation. We are like His name. Each one of us as individuals and all of us as a group make up His name [e.g., Almighty-Love-Healer-(fill in your name)-Counselor-Father-Patience-(fill in the name of anyone you know)-Provider-Savior-Redeemer-(fill in someone else's name)-Friend-Helper-Comforter-etc.]. Each person has a unique place and purpose in describing God. You have your place and purpose, and so does everyone else. When you're married, you and your spouse are right next to each other. You are important as individuals, but your union has a synergy that has its own purpose and power. When you try to be or do more than what the Lord created you to be or do, you weaken your position and contaminate the position of other people, thus distorting the Name and weakening His Body. This revelation was wonderfully freeing for me. All I had to do in life was be Lenore. No more, no less. God has given me all I need for this life and godliness (2 Peter 1:3).

We are all uniquely designed to fulfill a personal purpose. The main outcome of that purpose is to enhance the reputation of Jesus. He has given us His written word, the Bible, His Holy Spirit, and fellow earth travelers to guide us in that unique path. The fullness of the peace we are all striving for grows as we follow these guides. Our true selves begin to come out of hiding. We are more and more able to live according to the design that we were fashioned in before creation.

Following is a poem that sort of popped out of my pen one morning while I was journaling. I hope it speaks to your heart connects you with Jesus in some way.

I Am Not God After All

I have run away.
He revealed Himself to me
and it was too much for
my fragile ego.
I am not God after all.

I have run until I am cornered.
I have pawed and snarled
and climbed the walls
only to find that the strength
I depended upon
was an illusion.

I am not God after all.

It is time to stop
and turn around to the Hand
that is gentle and kind
and wants to take care of me.
He is God. He is Papa.

So I crawl into His lap and
He kisses my bruises and cleans the wounds,
and holds me
and the weight of all my sorrows.
He is God. And I am daughter.

He prepares a table for me
in the presence of my enemy.
I surrender.
He forgives.
He is God. And I am His.

APPENDIX 1

Attachment

HUMAN BEINGS WERE created with a need for relationship. The development of our brains, our minds and our physical well-being is dependent on interaction with others.

"The brain becomes literally constructed by interaction with others. ...our most intimate personal processes such as self are actually created by our neural machinery that is, by evolution, designed to be altered by relationship experiences." [1]

In our early years of development, implicit (subconscious), emotionally charged core beliefs about ourselves are created and set as foundation stones in our belief systems about ourselves and the world around us[2]. Moreover, according to Anne Halley, DMin. "The early development of the brain occurs as a result of the primary attachment relationship with mother." Before birth the child receives communication from the mother's voice and emotional state. The child is not capable of logically processing the information, and therefore stores it as emotional information. After birth the attachment style of the mother is the single most influential factor that determines how the child attaches or relates to other humans.

We were designed and created to develop in response to another. The early development of the brain occurs as a result of the primary attachment relationship with mother. ... The frontal brain of the infant is not fully developed at birth. The capacity to think has not yet been developed. [Therefore, t]he limbic system functions to the extent that *feelings associated with events are registered and later become founda-*

tions for thoughts. The immature brain does not have the capacity to adjust to stress and return to homeostasis or wellbeing. Soothing, calming, securing, understanding through eyes, touch, voice creates the "hook-up" for adjustment to stress. Neural pathways develop in response to the "hook-ups". The growing, developing and becoming "me" initially develops in here-and-now attachment relationship(s) with my mother (primary caregiver(s)) and later with others and my world." Anne Halley, D.Min. Formational Counseling Class notes.

God is passionate about relationship with us. When Jesus died on the cross, the first thing that happened was that the curtain in the Temple that separated the congregation from the presence of God was torn from top to bottom. The separation between the presence of God and His people was eliminated. Here are two definitions of human purpose:

Roman Catholic, Baltimore Catechism: Why did God make us? God made us to show forth His goodness and to ***share*** with us His everlasting happiness in heaven.[3]

Westminister Shorter Catechism: Man's chief end is to glorify God, and to ***enjoy*** him for ever.[4]

Emphasis mine. Notice how both definitions rely on interaction with God. Relationship. It is arguably our greatest need and at least as important as food and shelter.

Moreover, a study of 1,377 people found that the single related cause for mental illness, hypertension, malignant tumors, coronary heart disease and suicide was the lack of closeness to parents, especially the father.[5] When the father is in the home, the child is more capable of handling stress. According to Raj Chetty—the preeminent researcher on the topic of social mobility—having fathers in the neighborhood is a primary factor in predicting upward income mobility for the children in that neighborhood later in life, even when controlling for other variables such as the available schools, race, or ethnicity.[6] The need for relationship to our earthly father is a picture of our need for relationship to our heavenly Father. When He/he is nearby and part of our lives we have a better chance of thriving.

Style of attachment influences current relationships and is the number one factor in determining how a person's offspring behave in relationship.[7] In order to understand how attachment style influences relationship (i.e., how we love), let us look at the four different types of attachment: secure, avoidant, anxious and fearful. Bartholomew's Model of Self and Other provides a synopsis of how the styles compare with each other.

	SELF — POSITIVE VIEW Low Anxiety	SELF — NEGATIVE VIEW High Anxiety
OTHER — POSITIVE VIEW	SECURE *comfortable with intimacy and autonomy*	ANXIOUS *preoccupied with relationships and abandonment*
OTHER — NEGATIVE VIEW	AVOIDANT *down-plays intimacy, overly self-reliant*	FEARFUL *fearful of intimacy, socially avoidant*

Source: K. Bartholomew, "Avoidance of Intimacy: An Attachment Perspective", *Journal of Social and Personal Relationships*, 7(1990):174.

Secure Attachment

> "Secure attachment relationships in childhood and psychotherapy help develop this *reassuring internal presence* by providing us with experience of being recognized, understood, and cared for that can subsequently be internalized."[8]

One powerful factor in secure attachment is the internal, implicit sense that there is someone bigger than us who is taking care of us. If the child's life is filled with experiences that convince her that she is loved, safe, significant (she matters), and has purpose, understanding and belonging, the child will develop an implicit sense of self that is secure in herself and able to enter into relationships that reflect those core longings. "The essence of secure adult attachment with others and with God is the ability to understand our lives."[9] M. Pallner says, "People who believe they have a relationship with a stronger, wiser nonphysical deity report higher levels of global happiness."[10] We accomplish attachment by using a combination of implicit and explicit memory in this journey of understanding. It is critical in the healthy mode of relationship. Unhealthy attachment styles sabotage understanding and are a counterfeit of how to give and accept love.

In the Christian narrative, apart from Jesus all humans are without hope, because in and of ourselves we don't have the blamelessness that will allow passage into heaven or eternal peace. Our brokenness and the subsequent behaviors resulting from that brokenness (sin) make us unfit to be in God's presence. Much of our bad behavior comes from the lack of a reassuring internal presence. This implicit lack of reassurance can result in anxiety, self-hatred or depression, anger, etc.

Enter: repentance (changing the direction of your life to live in communion with God and thus according to His plan for us), and God's Holy Spirit.

Repentance has two parts: (1) acknowledging that we need deliverance from the sin (wrong living and separation apart from God) and (2) turning to Jesus/God to provide the deliverance. When you do that, Jesus fills us with His Holy Spirit, cleanses us from the sin, and gives us eternal life and hope (1 John 1:9). A divine, eternal reassuring internal presence enters us. Literally. It is actually the presence of God that comes to live in Christians.[11]

I know that can sound a little creepy. Sort of like our bodies get invaded by an alien presence, which is exactly right in a way. God is a separate type of being from us. He is self-sufficient and self-possessing. He doesn't need us or our belief in Him in order to exist. He just is, was, and always will be. As a human, we have this shadow of death hanging over us all the time. We know we have a birthday and we implicitly know we have an end. It is difficult to fathom a being that has no beginning or end. But that is God.

As I have stated previously, our parents and/or closest caregivers are the primary sources of our sense of self and consequently our belief of who God is. This sense of self doesn't exist on its own. It is deeply connected to, and some would say rooted in, the emotional foundations created in childhood experiences. Compared to knowledge, emotional experience is a stronger influence in creating our sense of self, because we experience life through our emotions. Our sense of self is saturated with the emotional content of our earliest experiences. Our parents help us to develop the reassuring internal presence by how they treat us, the environment they provide, how they nurture us (or not), how they relate to us as individual persons vs. projects, extensions of themselves, or objects on which to vent their emotions, etc. What our parents provide, regardless of how perfect they are as parents, is human interpretation. Parents are merely human and broken by sin that is inherent in human nature. Therefore, what they provide can never be enough to fully satisfy the souls of their children. At some point in our development, it is natural to discover that our parents are not God (or god, if you will) after all, and we must look elsewhere for fulfillment and contentment. I believe this is by God's design. It is His way of calling us to Himself.

When I was in seminary, I was part of a group called "Love, Healing and Development" led by Anne Halley, D.Min. One of the exercises was to picture in our imaginations our personal moment of conception; not in the carnal sense, but what was happening spiritually. What I learned was that God in all His intentionality chose one sperm out of the billions my dad produced, and out of the 100s of eggs my mother had, He chose one. He put them together to make me. He knew He needed the DNA from my particular mother and father to make a particular person that is Lenore. He also knew that the DNA in that egg and sperm was just about all that my parents had to give me. They provided an example of hard work and moral conscience, but very little regarding care for my soul. But what they had to give was enough. He would provide for the rest of my heart's needs. He knew the family I was placed in, the birth order I held, the community I would grow up in, all of it. It was His plan for the journey He had mapped out for me. The plan where He and I together could write the testimony that would show off some of His particular attributes through a particular me. In that moment of conception, that teeny tiny little Lenore had all she needed for life and godliness in Jesus. All the core longings (love, safety, significance, purpose, understanding, belonging) were waiting to be tapped into in Jesus (2 Peter 1:3) when I turned my life toward Him.

At that moment Jesus showed me that what my parents had for me was enough. In my imagination I could see them and experience them walking away into eternity together. I was released from the debilitating expectation that they were the source that would meet my deepest core longings. They just didn't have what I needed. Expecting them to meet my needs was like going to a dry well with a bucket for water and being disappointed each time. But Jesus has the water of eternal life. By inviting Him into those places of hurt and pain that were created by my needs not being met, the saving power of redemption in Jesus is displayed and Jesus is honored (see 2 Corinthians 12:9). I am still discovering places of hurt and pain where Jesus needs to enter and heal. It is the human journey.

John 15:1 and following talks about how Jesus is the "vine" and we are the "branches." "Apart from me, you can do nothing." Loosely interpreted, without attachment to Jesus, your life's purpose is thwarted.

I have included explanations of the unhealthy attachment styles in order for you to get an idea of where you fit on the Bartholomew's model above. It will help you determine what lie or lies you may be believing about yourself in relationships or in your world in general.

Avoidant Attachment

This is another way of loving, which downplays intimacy and is overly self-reliant. The person operating in this attachment style has a positive opinion of him/herself, but a negative opinion of everyone else.

His/her inner voice says, "Yes, I am worthy. No, these people don't really care about me."[12] This type of attachment is developed when parents stimulate exploration but interpret the child's pleas to reconnect as manipulation or weakness.[13] Imagine little Michael given the permission to go play and try out a new toy. He gets hurt or frightened by his playmates. When he runs to the parent he is misunderstood and turned away. His present need for comfort and safety is denied. He receives the message that these people don't love me. Moreover, it is easy to for him to take the message to the next level that says, "I am not safe with these people; therefore, I can't trust these people or, by extension, anyone." The "I am" descriptors that we use to describe ourselves (implicit or explicit) hold the most power over our sense of self and the world we live in.

One powerful way to overturn this unhealthy way of attachment is to determine to love first. If you believe people don't really care about you, don't allow that belief to be the basis of your relationship. Decide to love others regardless of how they react to you. If they are violent toward you in any way (body, soul or spirit), then set good boundaries. You are not required to put yourself in harm's way. However, we are required to love, to value and not devalue each other, even if it means loving each other according to the simplest premise that he/she is a human being created in God's image.

Check your pride at the door. A friend of mine, Pete Kuiper, offers this definition of pride: having an expectation of yourself or God that is not God's expectation. Is your expectation of yourself different from God's? Do you think of yourself more highly or lowly than you ought? Do you have an exaggerated sense of worth or deprecation? Do you compare yourself to others and find them or yourself wanting? It is likely that this comparison and the conclusion forms an important factor in your sense of self (1 Peter 5:5; Proverbs 3:32).

Pride is sneaky. It is evidence that our sense of self is fragile. Pride and shame are two heads of the same hydra. Shame drives pride to alleviate and/or mask the pain of self-hatred. Ironically, pride denies the true worth of a person, which is based on God's expectations. Pride sets up the person for a life riddled with shame, always trying to live up to a standard whose goalposts are always moving. Failure is inevitable. I've seen people create their own goals/self-righteousness so they don't have to try to meet these standards. See Ellen's story below. The problem is that the standards are counterfeit, invented by some caregiver/parent/authoritative influence whom the person heard as the voice of God when the expectation wasn't God's at all. The failure to meet the delusion is debilitating. The result is bitterness toward God. The solace found within the walls of bitterness becomes preferable to the risk of believing something different about God's expectation and who you are. A huge investment is made in the person's sense of self, which has been derived through these false expectations (pride). To trade them for a better understanding of self and God is to enter into a place where there was no sense of self at all. And that is a very scary place indeed. To give up the prideful creation of yourself would mean embarking on a risky journey where there was no guarantee that God or anyone else would show up for you. It's less painful to rely solely on oneself.

The answer is to embark on a journey of humility. My definition of humility: knowing you are in Christ, and knowing who He is in you, and living it without apology. It's a risky journey to give up all your ideas about yourself and God and be open to new revelations, but it will free you, give you permission, if you will, to be yourself. It will give you peace.

Ellen's Story

Ellen (fictitious conglomeration of several acquaintances of mine) grew up in a Christian home with a mother who was the daughter of an abusive alcoholic and a loving father that didn't stand up to the mother's negligence. Ellen never understood why her mother didn't like her. The mother had even told Ellen that if the mother had to choose between Ellen and her other siblings, she wouldn't choose Ellen. While the parents provided physically for the children, there wasn't much emotional connection, especially with the mother. After 50 plus years of trying to live up to the perceived Christian expectations of her community, Ellen decided she had had enough. She declared that Christianity doesn't work. God doesn't keep His promises. God isn't who the Bible and the church say He is. Ellen's anger and bitterness toward God was palpable. Her confession was that she liked herself, but she couldn't understand why people did not seem to want to be around her. She admitted she was critical and judgmental, but it was her way of dealing with the truth.

Ellen's lack of maternal connection and rejection created a deep sense of self-hatred that she denied. She had spent a lifetime trying to meet the expectations set before her and was faced with constant failure. The answer was to shut herself up in bitterness and soothe her pain with the prideful conclusion that she knows best. Whether the expectations or the failure were real didn't matter at this point. Ellen's hope for the future was departing from this world altogether.

Ellen's fear of taking the risk into a journey of self-discovery and new revelation of God prohibited her from the chance of peace that comes from living life in the fullness of her true self, who she is in Christ and who He is in her.

Anxious/Ambivalent Attachment

In the anxious/ambivalent attachment style the person has a negative view of him/herself and an unrealistic positive view other people. His/her belief is that "people around me really care," but "I'm not worthy of love." This scenario causes the person to be constantly checking to see if he/she is okay in the current situation or relationship. Two core longings that are attacked in this belief system are belonging and significance. Do I matter enough to be a part of my world?

The anxiety produced stems from a fear of abandonment developed in the first five years of life. The parents or caregivers were likely inconsistent, unavailable, or nonexistent with attunement to the small child. When the child cried for help or went to the caregiver for attention, the caregiver failed to interact (e.g., too busy with a cell phone, too busy with another sibling, distracted by [fill in the blank]) or forced the child to interact when the child wasn't interested. In other words, the parent/caregiver interacts with the child in order to meet the caregiver's needs versus attuning to and satisfying the needs of the child. When this happens, the child's natural attachment mechanisms are confused and thwarted. The result is anxiety that the child naturally tries to alleviate by flight or fight. This reaction is evident in anxiously attached children by the child reacting to a returning caregiver by hitting, ignoring or running away.

The anxiously attached live in constant fear of rejection. This creates a love bank that can never be satisfied, resulting in a person who is clingy. This leaves the person fragile and vulnerable to any perceived criticism, which is readily interpreted as rejection. Unfortunately, this longing for love from others and the debilitating lack of confidence in their own power of relating drives others away and serves as evidence that their fears of rejection are valid. Engaging in servitude may be another way to alleviate a sense of not belonging and unworthiness. The need for connection is met in the common activity rather than actual interaction with the people involved.

This lack of safety in relationship undermines the person's ability to engage in true intimacy. Deep intimacy, or heart-to-heart connection, is what humans long for. The anxiously attached live in fear of saying the wrong thing that will harm their frail sense of relationship. Without this connection and with the lack of confidence in their value and place in their world, the anxiously attached live in a world void of emotional stability. They look to authority figures to fix their problems and take care of them. They are convinced that they are not competent to make it on their own.[14]

One trap that people with this attachment style fall into is comparison. Do I measure up? I'm not talking about looking to someone for inspiration to be better in order to grow into God's plan for you. Rather I mean comparison that is based in covetousness or wanting to be another person other than yourself or comparison that is rooted in self-hatred. Don't get me wrong. Sometimes our lives become so engrossed in bad behavior that the behavior and consequent life situation seems like it is "me." Is "me" the life that you have created out of your sinfulness, or is "me" the eternal being that God saw before the foundations of creation (see Psalm 139 for the answer)? It's a very difficult thing to give up an existence that has been your own creation. You can be heavily invested on many levels: power, finances, intellectualism, culture, relationships. Are you willing to give up being the creator and embrace being the creature of a being who is Love? It means abdicating the throne of your self-created life and surrendering to your Creator. It's a simple solution but hard to carry out.

If you relate to this type of attachment style, it will take some work to rewire your brain and belief system. You can start by imagining yourself in a perfectly safe place and letting yourself experience the safety created. A funny thing about our imaginations is that our bodies don't know that what we are imagining is not physically real. So as you imagine being safe, your body will feel safe. As the experience of safety invades your body, you will eventually begin to feel more naturally at peace in everyday life and more comfortable with yourself and others. It's a good idea to do this exercise at least once a week or once a day. When you're ready, invite Jesus into your safe place and enjoy His presence there. Talk to Him. He's not afraid of anything you say or do. He loves you where you are and will give you wisdom for your life. It just takes practice. Again, the accepting presence of Jesus will realign your damaged belief system. You will begin to believe and live in the truth that no one is perfect. We are all part of the same imperfect human race; who you are is uniquely important in creation as is everyone else. You are enough. You belong.

Fearful Attachment

People with a fearful attachment style have a negative opinion of themselves and others. The narrative they live by is, "No, I am not worthy of love," and "No, others are not capable of loving me." As a result they have difficulty with intimacy and closeness, and often avoid relationships altogether. Like anyone, they long for real relationship. However, they are terrified of engaging at any level of closeness. When they work up the courage to launch out, their neediness tends to drive people away. They are fragile, easily shattered and vulnerable to any perceived offense. Their lack of confidence in their ability to engage and their lack of experience in real relationship supports the belief that they are not capable of doing life well.

People with fearful attachment frequently come from families that are abusive, where their source of comfort is also their source of pain. Severe cases of fearful attachment can result in dissociative behavior.[15]

Making Changes: Learning to Love

Have you ever been part of a demolition project, small or great? In the first blows against a fortified wall or structure you swing your hammer with all your might, and nothing seems to happen to the target. The energy of the swing runs back into your hands and arms and body. It can be painful. The same sort of thing can happen as we learn to love differently. Attachment styles are deeply rooted. You may be swinging against years, even generations, of patterns that are stubborn and don't change easily. Be encouraged. I don't know that love conquers all, but the love of God moving through us is certainly a powerful hammer against hard hearts, including (maybe especially) our own.

If you are reading this, chances are that you desire a deeper, truer existence that is filled with love and bathed in peace. Scripture promises perfect peace to the person who keeps his/her heart focused on the Lord (who is Love). I have experienced deep peace in moments with God. Futhermore, that peace has become more and more part of my everyday life during my nearly 40 years of walking with Him. There have been moments where the improvement has been incremental and moments where it has been a noticeable paradigm shift. We like to think that our lives grow in a straight line from salvation to heaven. In reality it's more of a circular path that sometimes ventures into very dark waters. Be assured that even in the dark places there is treasure to be had.[16] Jesus' final promise before He left into heaven was "I will be with you always..." (Matthew 28:20). In the final analysis, that's what it's all about.

EXERCISES FOR ATTACHMENT DISORDERS

1. Attend to the child within who never received the full attention he/she deserved. Dissemble the belief that you are not worthy of love by making a list of your most favorable assets. This could be a challenge if you're overwhelmed with the sense that you'll never be good enough. Start with generic truisms: I am a human and I am fearfully and wonderfully made (Ps 139). The fact that I'm alive is evidence that God has a plan for my life for today, for tomorrow, for next week, for the rest of my life; and He will guide me in it, even if I can't see it right now (Isaiah 30:21; Proverbs 3:5-6).

2. Learn to control your emotions and self-talk especially regarding relationships. Learn to use mindfulness techniques, controlled breathing, self-massage of arms and hands. Walk away when circumstances become too much to bear.

3. Resist the belief that relationships depend entirely on you and your behavior. Relationships take at least two people. You can't control anyone but yourself in a healthy relationship.

4. Learn to love first and let others be who they are. Love them as they are or love them and leave them. Just love them, with no expectation of love returned. When love is offered, acknowledge it and receive it even if you don't feel it. When you do this, you begin to surround yourself with an atmosphere of love that is safe and inviting versus an atmosphere of fear that demands love.

NOTES

[1]Marion F. Solomon and Daniel J. Siegel, *Healing Trauma: Mind, Body, and Brain*; W. W. Norton & Company, Inc. New York, NY, 2003 page 18.

[2]Tim Clinton and Joshua Straub, *God Attachment: Why You Believe, Act and Feel the Way You Do About God*; Howard Books; a div. of Simon & Shuster, Inc., NY, NY 2010, page 57.

[3]https://www.catholicity.com/baltimore-catechism/lesson01.html

[4]https://thewestminsterstandard.org/westminster-shorter-catechism/

[5]Tim Clinton and Joshua Straub, *God Attachment: Why You Believe, Act and Feel the Way You Do About God*; Howard Books; a div. of Simon & Shuster, Inc., NY, NY 2010, p. 53.

[6]Institute for Family Studies, https://ifstudies.org/blog/family-breakdown-and-americas-welfare-system, Dec. 4, 2020.

[7]Tim Clinton and Joshua Straub, *God Attachment: Why You Believe, Act and Feel the Way You Do About God*; Howard Books; a div. of Simon & Shuster, Inc., NY, NY 2010, page 6.

[8]David J. Wallen, *Attachment in Psychotherapy*, Gulliford Press, A Division of Fuilford Publications, Inc., New York, NY 2007, page72.

[9]Tim Clinton and Joshua Straub, *God Attachment: Why You Believe, Act and Feel the Way You Do About God*; Howard Books; a div. of Simon & Shuster, Inc., NY, NY 2010, page 57.

[10]M. Pollner, "Divine Relations, Social Relationships, and Well-Being," *Journal of Health & Social Behavior*, 30(1989): pages 92-104.

[11]Only those persons who are indwelt with the Holy Spirit are children of God. See John 1:12.

[12]Tim Clinton and Joshua Straub, *God Attachment: Why You Believe, Act and Feel the Way You Do About God*; Howard Books; a div. of Simon & Shuster, Inc., NY, NY 2010,page 72).

[13]Ibid. page 73.

[14]Ibid. pages 67-71.

[15]Ibid. pages 67, 73-74.

[16]Psalm 45:3: "I will give you the treasure of darkness and hidden riches of secret places." Psalm 139:12c: "The darkness and the light are both alike to you." NKJV

APPENDIX 2

The Reactive Cycle Fear Dance

(Adapted from Fight Your Way to a Better Marriage, *by Dr. Greg Smalley)*
Permission to use from CrossRoads Counseling of the Rockies

THE DESTRUCTIVE DANCE that frequently happens in conflicted relationships usually stems from a deep-seated emotional wounding that taps into significant fears held by the persons in the relationship. Every person struggles with at least one and usually several core fears that then become "hot buttons." The two most common core fears have to do with:

Loss of power

- the fear of helplessness,
- feeling controlled,
- fear of failing,
- being inadequate, or
- not being respected.

and...

Loss of connection with others

- the fear of not being understood,
- not being valued or affirmed,
- of feeling unloved, or
- of being alone.

What does the "Reactive Cycle Fear Dance" look like?

Identifying your core fear is important because it is the "musical cue" that starts your part of the relationship dance. When you are triggered, you react in ways that are designed to prevent the other person from causing you to feel ***your*** core fear. But the other person is rarely trying to trigger your defensiveness. That person is simply the instrument God is using to reveal a core fear that stems from a wound He wants to heal in you. In reality (if you are open to seeing it), the other person is actually giving you an opportunity to choose a better course of action that will allow you to deal with your core fear in a more healthy manner.

What are the steps in the "Reactive Cycle Fear Dance"?

In essence, the cycle begins when another person does something that "causes" you to feel hurt, anxious, disrespected, belittled, invalidated or some other emotional pain. You naturally want to stop feeling that pain. You want the other person to stop treating you in such as way that "causes you" to feel pain. You fear they won't stop, so you react in a way to try to motivate them to change. In doing so, you trigger the self-protective reactions in the other person. They feel hurt, threatened or exposed in regard to their core fears and so they react. And the dance begins. Most often, the issues that started the conflict are not the real problem. And the real solution is to be found in resolving your core fear or hot button issues.

Take a closer look at your "Reactive Cycle Fear Dance."

Use a separate piece of paper to write the answers to the following.

1. **Someone does something that triggers you.** Describe a recent conflict or negative situation with another person that really pushed your buttons/triggers. What did they do, or say, or what are they failing to do? Write about what happened:

2. **You hurt.** What does your hurt look like? What are the strongest emotions you feel when you are wounded like this? (Use the Emotional Pain Words on page 135). List the 3 or 4 strongest of those feelings:

3. **You interpret.** How did what happened during the conflict make you feel about yourself? What did you believe it said about you? What message was being received by you? What did the person's words or actions or failure to act mean to you? Every hot button is connected to a lie, false belief, or negative message that you have already believed about yourself. When this happened, I believed:

4. **You fear.** You want to connect, be accepted, respected, etc., but you feel threatened and fear the other person will not change in ways that reduce your pain. What do you fear the most? (See **Common Core Fears** list on page 136).

5. **You react.** What do you usually do when your buttons get pushed? How do you react when you feel that way? People fall into patterns of reacting when their "hot buttons" are pushed. Most people have ineffective reactions as they try to limit or manage their fears. As a result, our relationship are sabotaged. Every reaction will then be fight or flight.

> **Fighters** "engage" the other person when there is conflict in order to win or regain control. Fighters use things like escalation, angry outbursts, intimidation, criticism, sarcasm, debating, belittling comments, defensiveness, or fix-it mode to win an argument or to feel less threatened.

Flighters "disengage" from the other person when there is conflict, or withdraw when the conversation becomes difficult. Flighters use things like stuffing their feelings, avoidance, withdrawal, isolation, minimizing problems, or even spiritualizing to end an argument or to get what they want.

How do you react when you are threatented? What do you usually DO? (See **Reactive Coping Strategies** on pages 137 and 138.)

6. **Break the rhythm of the Fear Dance.** Once you identify your core fear and your reactive strategies, the solution often becomes much more clear. The best solutions start with realizing that your fears are just that—your fears. It is not primarily about changing the other person, but about you. It's about your own wounds, your own fears of further wounding, your own reactive strategies to try to avoid further pain. In other words, take ownership of what is yours to deal with. Being aware of and owning your core fears or hot buttons can help you recognize the lies and false beliefs that they are connected to and how they are in turn fueling your reactiveness. Renouncing the false beliefs with God and receiving His Truth will result in greater freedom and resolution, enabling you to "disconnect" the hot buttons. As a result, you can then be much more objective in addressing problem areas in the relationship.

So what might you do to ***respond*** differently vs. ***reacting*** the way you have in the past?

Emotional Pain Words

abandoned	accused	afraid	all my fault
alone	always wrong	angry	anxious
apathetic	ashamed	bad	belittled
betrayal	betrayed	bitter	blamed
can't do anything right	can't trust anyone	cheap	cheated
condemned	confused	conspired against	controlled
cut off	deceived	defeated	defenseless
defrauded	degraded	desires were rejected	despair
destroyed	devalued	didn't belong	didn't measure up
dirty	disappointed	disgusted	disrespected
dominated	embarrassed	empty	exposed
failure	fear	foolish	forced
frustrated	good for nothing	guilty	hated
hate myself	helpless	hollow	hopeless
humiliated	hurt	hysterical	impure
inadequate	indecent	inferior	insecure
insensitive to my needs	insignificant	invalidated	left out
lied to	lonely	lost	made fun of
manipulated	mindless	mistreated	misunderstood
molested	neglected	no good	not being affirmed
not cared for	not cherished	not deserving to live	not listened to
not valued	opinions not valued	out of control	overwhelmed
pathetic	pressured	pressure to perform	publicly shamed
rejected	rejection	repulsed	revenge
ruined	sad	scared	secluded
self-disgust	shamed	stressed	stupid
suffocated	suicidal	taken advantage of	thwarted
torn apart	trapped	trash	ugly
unable to communicate	unaccepted	uncaring	uncared for
unchosen	unclean	unfairly judged	unfairly treated
unfit	unimportant	unlovable	unloved
unnecessary	unprotected	unsafe	unsympathetic
unwanted	used	violated	vulnerable
wasted	wicked	worthless	wounded

Common Core Fears (Hot Buttons and Triggers)

Write a number from 0 to 5 in front of each common core fear, indicating how strongly you react internally when you feel threatened in that way.

____ 1. Helpless, powerless, impotent

____ 2. Rejected

____ 3. Abandoned

____ 4. Alone or don't belong

____ 5. Failure

____ 6. Unlovable

____ 7. Defective

____ 8. Inadequate

____ 9. Belittled

____ 10. Ignored

____ 11. Cheated

____ 12. Invalidated or devalued

____ 13. Unfulfilled or discontent

____ 14. Humiliated

____ 15. Manipulated

____ 16. Insecure

____ 17. Disrespected

____ 18. Controlled

Other(s)

Reactive Coping Strategies

Fight

____ 1. Escalate

____ 2. Become critical or judgmental

____ 3. Blame

____ 4. Angry outbursts

____ 5. Belittle

____ 6. Intimidate or threaten

____ 7. Counter-attack

____ 8. Become passive-agressive

____ 9. Get defensive

____ 10. People-pleasing

____ 11. Control or micromanage

____ 12. Stonewall

____ 13. Rescue or fix

Other(s)

Flight

____ 1. Withdraw or avoid

____ 2. Perfectionism

____ 3. Shut down, detach, or disengage

____ 4. Defense mechanisms (compartmentalize, dissociate, over-compensate, denial, etc.)

____ 5. Minimze

____ 6. Catastrophie or negatively interpret

____ 7. Self-pity or play the victim

____ 8. Self-medicate (drugs, alcohol, video games, TV, food, sleep, etc.)

____ 9. Intellectualize

____ 10. Complain

____ 11. Spiritualize

____ 12. Fantasize

____ 13. Need to be right

____ 14. Self-sufficient

____ 15. Isolate

____ 16. Stuff emotions

Other

What I want to feel in a relationship.

The following list may seem obvious. Take some time to acknowledge what your heart longs for most. It may be an indication as to what core longing(s) you most need to have filled.

____ 1. Loved and cared for*

____ 2. Connected

____ 3. Accepted and approved

____ 4. Competent*

____ 5. Understood*

____ 6. Significant or valued*

____ 7. Mutual trust

____ 8. Respected

____ 9. Desired

____ 10. Secure*

____ 11. Supported

____ 12. Belong, fit in*

____ 13. Validated

Other(s):

**Indicates a core longing.*

APPENDIX 3

Affirmations

This material was compiled from pages 218 through 242 in Growing Up Again *by Jean Illsley Clark and Connie Dawson, used by permission Hazeldon Publishing Company.*

Prenatal Stage: Becoming — Conception to Birth

Affirmations for Becoming

- I celebrate that you are alive.
- Your needs and safety are important to me.
- We are connected and you are whole.
- You can be born when you are ready.
- Your life is your own.
- I love you just as you are.

Stage One: Being — Birth to 6 months

Affirmations for Being

- I am glad you are alive.
- You belong here.
- What you need is important to me.
- I am glad you are you.
- You can grow at your own pace.
- You can feel all your feelings.
- I love you and I care for you.

Stage Two: Doing — 6 months to 18 months

Affirmations for Doing

- You can explore and experiment and I will support and protect you.
- You can use all of your senses when you explore.
- You can do things as many times as you need to.
- You can know what you know.
- You can be interested in everything.
- I like to watch you initiate, grow and learn.
- I love you when you are quiet and when you are active.

Stage Three: Thinking — 18 months to 3 years

Affirmations for Thinking

- I am glad you are starting to think for yourself.
- It is okay for you to be angry, and I will not let you hurt yourself or others.
- You can say no and push and test limits as much as you need to.
- You can learn to think for yourself and I will think for myself.
- You can think and feel at the same time.
- You can know what you need and ask for help.
- You can become separate from me and I will continue to love you.

Stage Four: Identity and Power — 3 years to 6 years

Affirmations for Power and Identity

- You can explore who you are and find out who other people are.
- You can be powerful and ask for help at the same time.
- You can try out different roles and ways of being powerful.
- You can learn the results of your behavior.
- All of your feelings are okay with me.
- You can learn what is pretend and what is real.
- I love who you are.

Stage Five: Structure — 6 years to 12 years

Affirmations for Structure

- You can think before you say yes or no and learn from your mistakes.
- You can trust your own intuition to help you decide what to do.
- You can find a way of doing things that works for you.
- You can learn the rules that help you live with others.
- You can learn when and how to disagree.
- You can think for yourself and get help instead of staying in distress.
- I love you even when we differ; I love growing with you.

Stage Six: Identity, Sexuality and Separation — 13 years to 19 years

Affirmations for Identity, Separation and Sexuality

- You can know who you are and learn and practice skills for independence
- You can learn the difference between sex and nurturing and be responsible for you needs, feelings and behaviors.
- You can develop your own interests, relationships, and causes.
- You can learn to use old skills in new ways.
- You can grow in your maleness or femaleness and still be dependent at times.
- I look forward to knowing you as an adult.

- My love is always with you. I trust you to ask for my support.

Adolescents make some of their identity and separation choices by revisiting or recycling the tasks of earlier stages. Therefore they may act very grown up one moment and immature the next.

Stage Seven: Interdependence — Adults

Affirmations for Adults

- Your needs are important.
- You can be uniquely yourself and honor the uniqueness of others.
- You can be independent and interdependent.
- Through the years you can expand your commitments to your own growth, to your family, your friends, your community and to all humankind.
- You can build and examine your commitments to your values and causes, your roles, and your tasks.
- You can be responsible for your contributions to each of your commitments.
- You can be creative, competent productive and joyful.
- You can trust your inner wisdom.
- You can say your hellos and good-byes to people, roles, dreams, and decisions.
- You can finish each part of your journey and look forward to the next.
- Your love matures and expands.
- You are lovable at every age.

APPENDIX 4

Forgiveness

Overview

THIS APPENDIX WAS created as a talk for my church's care ministry. It includes

1. What the Father's heart is regarding forgiveness and how important it is,

2. What forgiveness IS NOT,

3. What forgiveness IS,

4. The results of unforgiveness,

5. Steps to forgiveness.

The Father's Heart toward Forgiveness

Forgiveness is at the top of Jesus' priority list of why He came to earth. His mission was to reconcile us to the Father. Providing atonement and forgiveness for our sin was necessary for that to happen. When the apostles asked Jesus how to pray in Matthew 6:12-15, forgiveness was part of the answer:

> And forgive us our debts, as we forgive our debtors...For if you forgive men their trespasses, your heavenly Father will also forgive you. But if you do not forgive men their trespasses, neither will your Father forgive your trespasses. Matthew 6:12-15

Notice how our forgiveness from God is contingent on us forgiving others their trespasses. Another scripture teaching the same thing is the parable of the king and the two slaves:

> And his master was angry, and delivered him to the torturers until he should pay all that was due to him. So My heavenly Father also will do to you if each of you, from his heart, does not forgive his brother his trespasses." Matthew 18:34-35

Jesus on the Cross:

> "Father, forgive them, for they do not know what they do." Luke 23:34

Paul's letters:

> Let all bitterness, wrath, anger, clamor, and evil speaking be put away from you, with all malice. Ephesians 4:31

> Therefore, as the elect of God, holy and beloved, put on tender mercies, kindness, humility, meekness, longsuffering; bearing with one another, and forgiving one another, if anyone has a complaint against another; even as Christ forgave you, so you also must do. Colossians 3:12-13

Possible Reasons for Not Forgiving

1. Lack of time to deal with the emotion of it.

2. Lack of trust that the other party won't hurt me again.

3. You don't want to feel the pain again.

4. It takes a lot of effort.

5. Pride (having expectations of yourself or others that do not line up with God's expectations).

6. Guilt or shame (guilt: I DID something wrong; shame: I AM something wrong).

7. Fear.

8. Distraction or busyness.

9. Past unresolved pain from childhood.

What Forgiveness IS NOT

1. It does NOT mean condoning the behavior/offense, or that the offense was okay.

2. It does NOT mean excusing the behavior or saying it didn't matter.

3. It does NOT mean the offender cannot be held accountable if forgiven. The offender can be held legally responsible for his/her actions.

4. It does NOT mean the offender has to confess and repent before you forgive.

5. It is NOT mainly for the offender's benefit.

6. It does NOT mean you need to "forgive and forget," or ignoring the effects of the wrongdoing with the passage of time.

7. It does NOT mean you have to trust the offender. The wrongdoer is not necessarily trustworthy. Forgiving does not mean that you have to put yourself in harm's way.

8. It does NOT mean you have to reconcile with the offender. Romans 12:18 says "If it is possible, as much as depends on you, live peaceably with all men."

- Some people are no longer available through death or moving away.
- Reconciliation is a two-way street, and some people simply do not want to be reconciled.
- Forgiveness is mandatory; reconciliation is not mandatory.

9. It does NOT mean your feelings will automatically change.

10. It does NOT mean you need to tell the offender that you have forgiven them. Forgiveness is more than a verbal exchange. You may never have the opportunity to tell them. You may not need to tell them. Telling someone you have forgiven them can be a backhanded way of telling someone how hurt you are. No one needs to say "I forgive you," until they are asked to forgive.[1] (See Stephen in Acts 7:60; Jesus on the cross in Luke 23:34)

11. Forgiveness is not a quid pro quo (give and take) deal. The act of forgiveness doesn't demand compensation as a precondition. Forgiving also does not preclude seeking justice where appropriate.

Counterfeit Forgiveness

If forgiveness is easy you probably aren't forgiving, but rather offering a counterfeit forgiveness, such as

1. minimizing the offense,

2. excusing the offense, or

3. denial about the offense.

What IS Forgiveness?

1. It is a moral response to an injustice.

2. It is choosing to do good in the face of wrongdoing.

3. It is merciful restraint from pursing resentment or revenge, when the wrongdoer's actions deserve it. Forgiveness is letting God serve justice ("*Vengence is mine, I will repay*," says the Lord. Romans 12:19).

4. It is hoping for or contributing to the betterment of someone who has hurt you.

5. It is giving the gifts of mercy, generosity and love when the wrongdoer does not deserve them.

6. It is a freely chosen gift rather than a grim obligation.

7. It is the overcoming of wrongdoing with good.

8. It is releasing debt. (See the parable of the king and the two slaves, Matt 18:21-35.) The offender owes something: money, respect, love, protection, etc. You must release what you are owed and not give your offender what they deserve. You cannot cancel a debt that you do not acknowledge.

9. Forgiveness is removing barriers.[2] One of the most powerful avenues of forgiveness is when our perception is changed regarding ourselves, other people, or the circumstances.

10. It is giving up the hope of a better past.

The Nature of Forgiveness

1. Forgiveness abolishes the wall of wrongdoing between the two parties. (God/Person, Person/Person). The evil act is no longer a barrier to the relationship. The character of the offender can be a barrier to the relationship–he/she may not be trustworthy.

2. Christian forgiveness is unique in that it depends on God and our response.

God's forgiveness to Mankind is based on the cross of Christ, is offered to everyone, provides the opportunity to restore relationship with God, and is power for freedom to those weighed down by brokenness and guilt.

Believers are empowered by the cross and resurrection to forgive. God supplies the power to forgive. Forgiveness is a supernatural response empowered by God, which provides new hope for relationships with others.

3. In releasing the debt, you release your tie to the offender/debtor. If not, you are in bondage to the offense and the offender.

Unforgiveness

Unforgiveness is a type of self-defense mechanism, something we do to help make ourselves feel safe.

Lies sabotaging forgiveness

1. My unforgiveness continues to punish my offender.

2. I'm still in control when I don't forgive.

3. My offender must repent and feel remorse for me to forgive.

4. My unforgiveness protects me from my offender.[3]

Unforgiveness is described as eating poison and expecting our offender to die.

Consequences of unforgiveness:

1. The person unwilling to forgive is unable to experience God's forgiveness.

2. The unforgiving person becomes chained to the offender and the past offense like a ball and chain.

3. Repetition compulsion: you unconsciously repeat the same actions/thoughts over and over. This type of unforgiveness can create spiritual strongholds: ingrained, repetitive beliefs and/or thinking processes (neuropathways).

4. Generational sins: How we deal with circumstances and life, including holding grudges, can be handed down from generation to generation.

5. Increased tendency to develop a critical spirit (trying to protect yourself with judgment and criticism).

6. Giving control of your thoughts, attitudes, behaviors, etc. to the offender.

The natural progression of unforgiveness goes something like this: offended > bitterness > live in hurt > develop trust issues > fear people and close relationships > cripple support system > isolation/loneliness > depression > unforgiveness > bitterness > bondage

Steps to Forgiveness[4]

1. Recognize the offense and how you have been wounded.

2. Seek forgiveness for your part of the offense.

3. Renounce your rights to not forgive (no longer can justify harboring resentment).

4. Renounce your inner vows to not forgive.

5. Renounce the lie you have believed.

Woundedness can be grounded in truth OR your perception of the truth OR your own expectations. With expectations, unfulfillment arises out of the heart of the offended rather than from the actions of the offender. It doesn't matter if the expectations are legitimate or realistic—or not; if the expectations doesn't materialize we may become resentful or bitter. Forgiveness requires you to release your expectations regardless of their legitimacy. If expectations aren't met, you must decide if you want to be ruled by another person's failure.

Persons may need to grieve the loss of unfulfilled expectations or dreams. *Marriages can end due to the unforgiveness surrounding disappointed expectations.*)

After determining any lies you have believed from the offense, replace the lie with the Truth from Jesus. Matt. 12:43-45 says, "If you cast out an unclean spirit and don't fill the place it held, it will return with spirits more evil and in greater number."

6. Feel and release the emotions surrounding the offense (e.g., write a lament, engage in physical activity while you emote about the offense).

7. Make a conscious choice to forgive, even if the feelings of forgiveness are not there.

8. Release your offender into the hands of Jesus so that he/she will no longer have power over you.

My friend and colleague, Pete Kuiper, uses the analogy of a court when he describes forgiveness. You bring your offense into your court where you are the judge, jury, prosecuting attorney, and executioner. As you hold your file(s) containing the truth of the offense, you realize you cannot serve justice in love without revenge (Romans 12:19), so you hand your file to the Lord and ask Him to serve justice. And He will.

Keep in mind the words of John the Baptist, "Behold the Lamb of God who takes away the sins of the world." (John 1:29) Jesus not only takes away the sins we are guilty of, but He takes away the sin that has been sinned against us. We don't have to carry the sin of others. Jesus can take that, too. It is His glory to take on sin. He can handle it.

9. After you have consciously forgiven, build a stronghold of compassion to replace the bitterness.

Tearing Down the Stronghold of Bitterness[5]

Retaining an offense vs. releasing it is the first open door to bitterness. The question isn't "Will you be offended?", rather "Will you retain the offense or release it?" Bitterness and unforgiveness open up a door that gives the devil a place to operate from. In Ephesians 4:23-27 Paul writes, "In your anger do not sin. Do not let the sun go down while you are still angry, and do not give the devil opportunity." The word "opportunity" means an area of legal control. Bitterness says, "I must punish my offender." God says, "Vengence is Mine, I will repay." Romans 12:19 God is just. Justice will be served. God can and will do it. How? That's His business.

Steps[6] to Tearing Down the Stronghold of Bitterness

1. Recognize that unforgiveness is sin (confess the sin).

2. Revoke the legal right for bitterness to remain – choose to forgive.

3. Regain: Ask God to regain the surrendered ground that gave a "foothold" or opportunity for bitterness to take root.

4. Remove the stronghold, and

5. Replace it with God's Truth about yourself, your offender, the circumstances, etc.

Key to Staying Free

Rebuild the area of unforgiveness with a godly stronghold of compassion. Matt 12:43-45 (Fill the evacuated space in your heart with God's Spirit and grace.)

1. Recognize that it is God's will that we forgive.

2. Meditate on God's forgiveness for you.

3. Receive grace to demonstrate mercy.

4. Love with God's love (love = to value and not devalue).

5. Live life free from offense. This is a challenge, because old wounds provide a place (triggers) for offenses to land.

When old feelings of unforgiveness return:

1. Review the forgiveness process.

2. Consider how actively are you pursuing a compassion stronghold?

3. You can sabotage your wholeness if you neglect building compassion.

A Few Words about Forgiving Yourself.

1. We do not have to make God willing to forgive. In fact, we are already forgiven. God is waiting patiently for us to acknowledge the work of the Cross and receive the grace and forgiveness that is readily available.

2. Pride is a strong opponent to forgiveness for yourself. Acknowledging that imperfection is part of being human is an important first step. Perfect people don't need Christ's forgiveness.

3. So often people think that if they can just feel bad enough about themselves or the situation, surely they can come to some point of relief. Condemnation and self-pity, which are forms of pride say, "if I (or the other person) suffer enough, surely there will be some release, or atonement." Ps 49: 7-9 states (paraphrase) that "No man can save his brother. Give up trying altogether." Most cultures have some tradition that provides atonement. God created us with the ability to recognize our need for atonement so that we would look to Jesus for it. True atonement can be found only in Jesus. Pride holds us back from completely embracing our hopelessness apart from Jesus' work on the cross.

NOTES

[1]Rodney Hogue, *Forgiveness*, Rodney Hogue, 2008, page 22.

[2]Kenneth D. Haugk, *Christian Caregiving, A Way of Life*, Stephens Ministries, St. Louis, 2012, page 82.

[3]Rodney Hogue, *Forgiveness*, Rodney Hogue, 2008, page 72

[4]Ibid. page 48.

[5]Ibid. pages 47-56.

[6]Ibid. pages 47-56.

[7]Ibid. Chapter 8.

APPENDIX 5

Love Bonds vs. Fear Bonds in Relationships

Love Bonds	Fear Bonds
1. **Based on love** and characterized by truth, closeness, intimacy, joy, peace perseverance and authentic giving.	1. **Based on fear** and characterized by pain, humiliation, desperation, shame, guilt, and/or fear of rejection, abandonment or detrimental consequences.
2. Bond is **desire driven**. (I bond because I want to be with you.)	2. **Bond is avoidance driven.** (I bond because I want to avoid negativefeelings or pain.)
3. Love Bonds **grow stronger both when we move closer *and* when we move farther away.** (When we move closer, I get to know you better. When we move farther away, I am still blessed by the memory of you.)	3. Fear Bonds only **grow stronger by moving closer *or* by moving farther away**. (The closer we get, the scarier it gets, so I have to avoid the closeness; or the farther away we get, the scarier it gets, so I have to manipulate closeness.)
4. **We can share both positive and negative feelings.** The bond is strengthened by this truthful sharing.	4. **We cannot share both positive and negative feelings.** The bond is strengthened by 1) avoiding negative or positive feelings, or 2) by seeking only negative feelings or seeking only positive feelings.
5. Participants on both ends of the bond benefit; the bond **encourages all to act like themselves.**	5. Participants on only one end of the bond gain advantage; the bond **actually inhibits people from acting like themselves.**
6. **Truth** pervades the relationship	6. **Deceit and pretending** are required.
7. Love bonds continually **grow and mature people**, equipping them to find their hearts.	7. Fear Bonds increasingly **restrict and stunt growth**, keeping people from finding their hearts.
8. Love bonds operate from the front brain (the joy center), and **govern "how do I act like myself?"**	8. Fear Bonds operate from the back of the brain, and **govern "how do I get what I want?"**

The Fear and Love Bonds are in the book Living From the Heart Jesus Gave You *by Dr. Jim Wilder et al, page 69. Cited here with permission from Life Model Works.*